MW01077765

A Hermit's Cookbook

A Hermit's Cookbook

*Monks, Food and Fasting
in the Middle Ages*

Andrew Jotischky

continuum

Continuum International Publishing Group

The Tower Building   80 Maiden Lane

11 York Road   Suite 704

London SE1 7NX   New York, NY 10038

Copyright © Andrew Jotischky, 2011

ISBN: HB: 978-0-8264-2393-1

Typeset by Pindar NZ, Auckland, New Zealand

Printed in the U.S.A.

Book Club Edition

Contents

Illustrations

To Caroline, Christopher, Clementine and Gabriel
– reluctant associates

Preface

Tell me what you eat, and I will tell you what you are.

Brillat-Savarin

Some people are interested in food, how it is prepared and where it comes from; some enjoy eating but pay little attention to how the food arrives on their plate; many are too busy to go to much trouble over it and settle for what is most convenient; a few people dislike food and the act of eating – but hardly anyone is utterly indifferent to food. We might have sophisticated or crude tastes in food and drink, and most people in the developed world have a much more varied diet than was the case several hundred years ago, but we all have active likes and dislikes.

This book is a culinary history of monasticism. That is to say, it is a whimsical history of monasticism: one that traces the history of Christian religious life through food, eating and fasting. More specifically, it is about the deliberate relegation of food and eating to a purely physical need, divorced from any sensation of pleasure or displeasure, on the part of individuals and communities who followed a religious life in the period from the earliest days of Christianity through to the late Middle Ages. It is about the ascetic spirit that governed such an attitude to food and eating, and about the kinds of food eaten by monks and hermits who tried to live in pursuit of this spirit. This book takes as its starting point an extraordinary phenomenon: indifference to food. It deals with historical characters who had trained both body and mind to accept and be content not only with very little food, but with food of very little variety or interest. One such character is the 'hairy anchorite' Onuphrios, a solitary monk in the Sinai desert who is reputed to have lived for most of his adult life on nothing but dates. Another example is Hilarion, like Onuphrios an early Christian, who set himself to follow a diet consisting of the same kind of food – first barley bread, then lentils, then soup – for years at a time without alteration. The twelfth-century monk Bernard of Clairvaux was so indifferent to what he ingested that his monks watched him drink from a cup filled with olive oil, under the impression that it was water, without apparently noticing the difference. A degree of practical abstinence from food and drink was a consequence of a set of ideals about the body and how to regulate it as part of a holy life. This book starts by dealing with a small minority who were able to turn those ideals into reality in their own lives. It will examine how such people lived, what they ate, and why they regarded abstinence from food and strict control of the body as a necessary part of the religious life – as an ideal to be sought and perfected.

This book is also about the impossibility of preserving that ascetic spirit once monastic life had become a fixed and flourishing part of the society that the first monks tried so hard to escape. Not all monks, nuns, hermits or friars deliberately cultivated indifference to food. The theme of the book is the constant tension between the monastic ideal and the social and economic realities that underlay religious life. If delighting in food is the opposite of indifference to it, this book is about compromise and failure as well as supreme achievement. In reality, most religious people, like most ordinary people then as now, probably took a healthy interest in their appetites. In the second half of the book, we will look at how monastic life increasingly came to mirror society outside the monastery, and thereby to lose the distinctiveness it had enjoyed in its early centuries.

*   *   *

My first visit to a monastery in the cradle of monasticism – the Near East – was in 1993, when I was touring places connected with my research into medieval monasticism in Jerusalem. I went

1.   Garden of St Gerasimus, near the banks of the River Jordan

to as many monasteries as possible that were open to pilgrims and visitors. Among these was the monastery of St George Choziba, perched on a narrow ledge halfway up a cliff in the wadi Qilt, between Jerusalem and Jericho. A twelfth-century pilgrim, John Phokas, describes the approach from the road as 'a place about which no report will be believed, and only when one sees it can one understand its wonders . . . the church and cemetery are set in the chasm of the rock, and everything is so blasted by the burning sun that one can see the rock emitting tongues of flame like pyramids.' Perhaps Phokas was letting his imagination run a little wild, but in the heat of a mid-September day in the Judaean desert one can appreciate his metaphorical language. Even so, the discomfort was worth the effort just to experience the stunning reality of the place.

My immediate impression was one of amazement that anyone *could* live in such a remote place, let alone that they would want to do so.

After looking around the austere buildings of the monastery, some of which testify to a rebuilding programme in the twelfth century, I sat down on a bench in the shade. There were no other visitors. One of the monks came and sat down beside me. He asked me where I was from, and told me a little about himself. Like many of the monks in the monasteries of the Jerusalem patriarchate, he was from one of the Greek islands. He went into one of the buildings and emerged with a basket filled with small cakes and fruit – figs, dates and grapes. 'We celebrated a holy feast yesterday,' he explained, 'and these are leftovers. Please eat.' As I did, he told me that the ancient custom of the monastery was to reserve a portion of festival food for pilgrims and travellers who might pass by. Feeding wayfarers was also, I remembered, a sacred rule of hospitality among the Greeks going back to Homeric times. The simple food set me thinking about the practicalities of living in such a monastery. Could anything possibly grow in such a parched landscape? Did all their supplies have to be brought in from outside? There was only a single track suitable for vehicles from the main road for transporting supplies.

After leaving the monastery, I walked along the wadi track to Jericho, a matter of only a few miles. Around Jericho, the land is flat and fertile, and the town is surrounded by orchards and fields. Another monastery near Jericho, St Gerasimus, which I also visited later, has extensive orchards and vegetable gardens of its own. But the wadi Qilt and the land to either side is rocky and dry. Walking along the track, however, it was possible to see signs of cultivation along the wadi bed. On subsequent visits to the Judaean desert in winter and spring, it became clear that for parts of the year, during the rainy season, it was indeed possible to grow fruit and vegetables in the Judaean desert. I also read studies of the desert monasteries by archaeologists that confirmed the existence of gardens and fruit groves here and in the Kidron Valley south-east of Bethlehem, where the great monastery of St Sabas perches in an equally remote location and an equally unforgiving landscape.

The question of monastic diet is, at one level, intensely practical. Any solitary monk or monastery in a remote area needs either to be self-sufficient in food production or to have ready access to a local economy that can provide food. At the same time, however, what monks and hermits ate is also a question that opens up another, more spiritual dimension. Contemporary accounts of holy men and women from the period spanning the origins of monasticism in the late Roman Empire to the Middle Ages show a particular interest in the ability of monks to survive on very little food. Indeed, this is one of the attributes of their holiness. Onuphrios and his diet of dates fits into a particular category of holy man: the desert monk who is so other-worldly that he can survive on practically nothing. We shall meet, in the course of this book, monks who refused to eat food that had been cooked, monks who ate only food that grew naturally without the need for cultivation, and others who ate only scraps and kitchen leftovers. How the practical business of feeding oneself or a whole monastic community relates to this spiritual dimension of ascetic eating is the subject of this book.

Acknowledgements

Writing a book always incurs debts, not all of which can be recognized easily. A number of mine are to people who had no idea, at the time, of how their helpfulness or expertise might feed into this book. Among these are Toby Macklin and Rachel Davey, who unwittingly cooked for me the perfect version of Orthodox monks' stew in Cyprus – possibly the starting point for this book. I am also grateful to the monks of Choziba, St Sabas and St Gerasimus in Israel/Palestine and to St John the Theologian in Patmos; to various friends and colleagues whom I have bored over the years; and above all, to my family for their patience and fortitude in (occasionally) agreeing to be experimented upon.

Note: We have very little evidence of how many of the foods described in this book were actually cooked. I have reconstructed the recipes included here to be plausible from a culinary standpoint, while attempting to preserve the integrity of the source material.

Chapter One

Beginnings – who were the first monks?

Throughout this book the term 'monk' is used fairly loosely to denote someone following a religious life, whether self-governing and alone or in a community. Properly speaking, 'monk' simply denotes someone who followed a monastic life, although since the derivation of the word comes from the Greek *monos*, meaning 'single' or 'alone', it was almost certainly applied first of all to solitaries whom we would tend to think of as hermits. In fact, although the literature of early monasticism certainly distinguished between solitary and communal monasticism as styles or forms of religious life, it saw the term 'monk' as applying to anyone leading such a life, whether alone or as part of a community. The religious life was fluid: monks might drift from solitary living to living in a small group of like-minded religious to a large and well-organized community.

The word 'hermit', etymologically, has nothing to do with being a solitary, although the sense in which we tend to use it evokes ideas of recluses living alone. The word comes from the Greek (and Latin) word *eremos*, meaning a 'wilderness' or 'desert'. However, the desert did not necessarily have to be literal: it might refer to the wilderness of solitude, or to self-imposed discipline on the part of the monk separating himself from society. Thus, for example, St Anthony is described as being a monk living in the desert even at the earliest stage of his withdrawal from society, when in all likelihood he was simply occupying waste ground not too far from his native village – and, of course, he is always called a monk in contemporary accounts, even though we might more naturally think of him as a hermit. As we shall see, medieval reformers also used the term 'desert' figuratively, even to apply to communal monks living in parts of the West such as Burgundy, which are very far from being deserts in the literal sense. 'Anchorite' is a more specific and technical term, and could only be applied to a solitary monk – alongside its female counterpart, 'anchoress'. In the later Middle Ages (from the thirteenth century onward), there was special ecclesiastical legislation for anchorites and anchoresses, and the term came to be applied specifically to men or women who had chosen to live as recluses in supervised conditions, usually in purpose-built cells attached to parish churches. However, for most of the period covered by this book, the term anchorite is simply an alternative to hermit or solitary monk.

The number of men and women who followed a religious life in the formal sense of belonging to a community or Order bound by rules was surprisingly large. We will never be able to estimate what proportion of society at any point lived in monasteries, but we do know that in the late Roman and early medieval periods, monasteries could house huge numbers of people. The monasteries founded by Pachomius in the fourth century near the Nile in Upper Egypt were designed for several hundred monks; they have often, rather glibly perhaps, been compared to Roman army barracks. Similarly, in eighth- and ninth-century France, monasteries could have housed a few hundred monks. The numbers diminished steadily, not necessarily because spiritual vocations dwindled, but rather because, by the mid-eleventh century and beyond, there were more options available for those drawn to such a life: more monasteries encompassing varying types of religious life and, from the twelfth century onward, more religious Orders and congregations from which to choose, some of which deliberately kept themselves very small. Even so, in the 1120s, the largest monastery in western Europe, Cluny, had about three hundred monks.

Many recruits, especially from about the tenth century onward, probably did not choose to become monks or nuns in the first place, but grew up in religious communities where they had been placed as children. This practice of 'oblation' – literally, an 'offering' to the monastery – was widespread in both the Greek Orthodox and

Western Churches during the Middle Ages, although it was criticized at various points by reformers. Although in theory oblates were free to choose to leave the monastery once they reached adulthood, in practice most probably stayed in the only environment that they knew. The reasons for oblation were partly cultural and partly socio-economic. Large families were difficult for even aristocratic households to maintain, so the prospect of one or two fewer mouths to feed was always welcome. Moreover, placing a child in a monastery meant that he or she would be guaranteed a level of material comfort and safety that could not always be assured in the outside world.

Furthermore, having a relative in a monastery, especially if he or she rose to become abbot or abbess, was valuable both politically and in terms of social prestige. Since monasteries in the Middle Ages were land-owning institutions, they often boasted rich endowments and property. This meant that the heads of such communities were powerful figures who enjoyed the same rights of local jurisdiction and the same political influence and obligations as secular lords. Placing a child in a monastery could be seen as a family investing in its own future. In a society in which primogeniture – the inheritance of all family property by the oldest son – was becoming the norm, giving a younger child to a monastery was tantamount simply to finding an alternative career path to that of landless knight, who would otherwise be a drain on the family resources, and who might in any case struggle to make a mark in the world. Children might be placed in monasteries as young as seven, though frequently it happened only when they had already reached the age of puberty. This practice doubtless seems overly deterministic to us, but we should remember that children of the nobility might equally be betrothed at the age of seven – life choices as we know them were far less available in the Middle Ages.

Contemporaries were aware of the potential psychological effects of the practice of oblation. Guibert of Nogent was twelve when his widowed mother retired to a convent; soon after, he became a novice. In later life, as abbot of the small monastery of

Nogent in northern France, he wrote a remarkable memoir of his life, in which he reflected on the advantages and disadvantages of oblation. He faced up squarely to the trauma his mother's choice on his behalf had caused him, although he acknowledged his suitability for the monastic life. He was grateful for the education that the monastery had given him – an opportunity not to be found in the lay society of his day. But at the same time he freely admitted his terror of the world outside the cloister – a world that seemed to him irredeemably evil, dangerous and full of misery. Oblation was for him both a blessing and a curse: it had kept him safe, made him a learned man and fulfilled his desire for study, but it had also made him a stranger in the world beyond the walls of his monastery. Most important, however, Guibert recognized, as most of his contemporaries did, that salvation was far more likely to be attained by those who lived a monastic life, for such a life offered far fewer opportunities for sinfulness, and more for virtue. Among the latter, of course, was a life of self-denial and abstinence from excess in food and drink.[1]

A BRIEF HISTORY OF MONASTIC ORIGINS

The first Christian monks appear in the sources in the third century. Fragments of papyrus from Egypt record the existence of men listed as *monachoi* in tax registers. The fact that they were known and could be counted suggests that they lived in or near settled habitations rather than in the desert. Despite these tantalizing glimpses of the earliest monks, monasticism is really a creation of the fourth century. In order to understand how and why it emerged, we must first examine how Christianity itself developed in this period, the era in which it emerged from the darkness to dominate cultural life in the Empire.

The Great Persecution, which had been instituted to eradicate Christianity, ended in the early years of the fourth century when the Emperor Diocletian realized that it was an impossible task. A few years later, Constantine, an obscure general from Britain, took over his father's role of Caesar (second in command of the Western Empire), and in AD 312 he marched on Rome to make himself Emperor of the West. At the battle of Milvian Bridge, in northern Italy, Constantine defeated the incumbent, Maxentius. This might have remained little more than one of the frequent trials of strength between those vying for imperial rule, were it not for Constantine's proclamation after his victory that, in consequence of a vision he had been granted on the eve of the battle, he had become a follower of the Christian God. He furthermore issued a decree – the Edict of Toleration – permitting Christian worship in public on equal terms with any other form of religious practice. There was nothing inherently surprising about this: in the early fourth century, perhaps ten per cent of the Empire's population was Christian, and the religion was regarded by most Roman citizens as simply one of a number of ways of worshipping the divine. Religion in the late Roman Empire was highly syncretistic, and many people thought that the divine could be worshipped in a number of different guises according to local traditions. Moreover, monotheism was not confined to Christians or Jews; it was a serious philosophical position held by Neoplatonists and others. However, Christianity had some features that distinguished it from other cults that had emerged from obscure corners of the Empire. One of these, as it transpired over the course of the next few centuries, was a spectacular intellectual adaptability. To an outsider, though, Christian practices and ethics must have looked very similar to those of a number of other religious cults and philosophical affiliations. Christian ethics, including views about the body, personal conduct, self-control and regulation of one's bodily appetites, were certainly neither original, nor unique. They were derived from Jewish ethical teaching, and informed by both Neoplatonic and Stoical philosophical traditions.

In the early fourth century, perhaps the most surprising feature of Christianity was the willingness of so many of its adherents to succumb to judicial torture and death at the hands of local civic and imperial authorities during the Great Persecution. This feature of Christianity also conferred a distinctive identity on those Christians who survived the Persecution. The memories of those who had refused to renounce the religion and died for it were venerated as martyrs – public witnesses to the faith. Their burial places became sites of special holiness, and the anniversaries of their deaths were commemorated in special liturgies. Once the Persecution was over, however, Christianity was no longer a dangerous faith. Indeed, imperial favour swung more and more towards it, as Constantine and his family built and endowed churches. In the 320s, after defeating the eastern Emperor Licinius and making himself sole ruler of the Roman world, Constantine became increasingly partial towards the Christian Church. He founded a new imperial capital, named after himself, in the east: Constantinople. Unlike Rome, which was heavily dominated by a senatorial aristocracy that was largely traditional in its religious outlook, the new city was blatantly and openly Christian. Christian bishops and advisors became the new political class of the Empire. The dangers to the faith itself, however, were obvious. Naturally, conversion to the favoured religion increased exponentially, especially in the eastern half of the Empire, as the benefits and rewards of being Christian became more obvious. But when there was no longer any need for Christians to resist the state authorities – when, indeed, Christianity became increasingly identified with the State itself – part of what had made Christians distinctive as a grouping within society disappeared. Christians no longer had to be revolutionaries who despised the world in which they lived and kept their eyes firmly fixed on the afterlife. In such circumstances, some Christian leaders worried that the discipline of the faith would be undermined.

There were other reasons why the success of Christianity posed challenges to the Church. Already by the early fourth century it had been apparent to bishops that it was impossible to reconcile the different styles of Christian worship and variations of belief that had developed independently of each other in different parts of the Roman world. Not until 325 was it possible to lay the foundations for a theology that could be universally held by all Christians. Even then, there was to be no facile agreement over the doctrines of the

Church. Christian teaching was argued over, debated and finally hammered out at a series of ecumenical councils, at which extreme theological positions were rejected and compromises sought. Some of these, such as that at Ephesus in 431 and Constantinople in 451, brought the major centres of the religion – Antioch, Alexandria, Rome and Constantinople itself – into head-to-head conflict, resulting in severe ruptures in the community of faith.

In such circumstances, the deaths of the early martyrs became an important set of spiritual compass points from which Christians could remind themselves of their original identity. For this reason, bishops, teachers and writers were keen to commemorate these martyrs, even long after their historical memories had disappeared. One of these influential teachers, Jerome, thought that monastic life in the later fourth century owed its origins to the period of the martyrdom: the first monks, he reasoned, must have been Christians who fled towns and cities to escape persecution and who settled in the desert because it was the only place they could hide from the authorities. This attempt to link monastic life of his day – the late fourth and early fifth centuries – with the period of martyrdom shows that a hundred years or so after Diocletian first instituted the Persecution, it was seen as a kind of golden age of Christian virtue, the period in which 'real' holiness had begun. The monks were the link to that golden age.

Monks, moreover, maintained the link by living lives of sacrifice. Just as the martyrs had given their lives in a single, final gesture of rejection of worldly values, so monks lived as witnesses to the same principle of rejection. They gave up everything when they embarked on the monastic life: comfort, ease, political and social status, the enjoyment of everything the world had to offer. They renounced their sexuality and their appetites in preference for lives of poverty, chastity and perpetual worship. In an age in which martyrdom was no longer a fact of life and Christianity not under threat, this was all that the truly virtuous had to give. The monks, then, were the successors of the martyrs.

There were, of course, many other ways of articulating the

origins of monasticism. A prominent Byzantine monk at the end of the eleventh century, John the Oxite (so called because he was a member of the Oxeia monastery in Constantinople), wrote that the first monks were simply members of the early Church who thought that the only way to worship God continually, and to place that worship above all other concerns, was to live in communities of like-minded people, away from the distractions of society. This may reflect one strand in monastic sentiment as it developed over the centuries, namely a distrust and dislike of the everyday concerns that have always preoccupied most people in any society. For example, the twelfth-century Cypriot monk Neophytos, looking back on his career as a reclusive monk later in life, admitted that he had decided to become a monk at the age of eighteen because he could not bear the thought of marriage, the troubles and cares brought by children and family life, or the worries of trying to make ends meet.

There were also more positive ways of looking at monastic life. John Cassian, writing in the early years of the fifth century, explained that the different kinds of monks derived from examples in the Scriptures. In his view, monks who lived as solitaries were imitating the example of the great prophets of the Old Testament, such as Elijah, who had wandered desolate regions in the course of their missions. Those who lived in monasteries under a rule, in contrast, were following the example of the first Christians of Jerusalem, who were described in the *Acts of the Apostles* as living in community and holding all their property in common. Cassian was trying to find a typological explanation for the meaning of monasticism, rather than tracing the actual historical origins of the phenomenon. His explanation proved to be highly influential, and the identification of biblical precursors for different type of religious life became standard throughout the Middle Ages. It reached its most baroque and inventive peak in Carmelite history in the fourteenth century – the Carmelites claimed that they were themselves the successors of the prophet Elijah, and that an unbroken line of hermits had lived on Mt Carmel ever since his day.

Egypt

So much for the theory of monastic origins; what about the historical reality? The traditional view is that the first monks, both solitary and communal, emerged in Egypt in the third century at about the same time but quite independently of each other. This view derives largely from one of the most influential pieces of writing of the late Roman period, indeed of Christian history: the *Life of Anthony*. Its author was the fourth-century bishop of Alexandria, Athanasius. The story told in this short work – it can easily be read from start to finish in little over an hour – established most of the features that were to become standard attributes of solitary holy men and women for centuries. Although Athanasius was a Greek speaker – Alexandria being a largely Greek-speaking city – and wrote in Greek, the *Life of Anthony* was translated into Latin in his own lifetime. This was a sign both of how influential it had become only a few years after its initial launch, and also of how important Athanasius saw it as a means of spreading the message he wanted to convey in the work. Athanasius regarded biography as the perfect vehicle for this message, and his Anthony, though probably a real enough historical figure, mirrored his view of how monks should live. Although short, it is far from being a straightforward narrative of Anthony's life; in fact, relatively few details of how Anthony spent his supposed one hundred and five years are provided.

We first encounter Anthony at the age of eighteen, as a newly orphaned devout Christian from Lower Egypt, a young man of considerable means but with a younger sister to support. Convinced that the best way to follow the teaching of Jesus was to give up his possessions, Anthony sold off the agricultural estate he had been left by his parents – probably about two hundred acres in extent – and all his portable property, and packed his young sister off to be looked after by a group of Christian women devoted to a life of virginity; in other words, nuns. He then went off himself to study the monastic life by seeking out virtuous men who practised asceticism in order to devote themselves to God. It is clear from the

context that there were already monks in the most heavily populated and fertile part of Egypt, that some lived alone and others in
associations or groups, that monks might be men or women, and
that they might live in or near villages and towns, or at a more
remote distance from them. Egyptian society in the late Roman
period clung to the Nile. As the ancient proverb said, Egypt was
the gift of the Nile: its prosperity came from the fertility of the land
in a narrow strip watered by the Nile, and especially from the delta
created by the fissuring of the great river into several tributaries
at its northern end, where it meets the Mediterranean Sea. It was
the flooding of the Nile every summer, which caused the river to
burst its banks and spread itself over the surrounding countryside,
that made this region so fertile. Anthony appears to have spent
several years living among or alongside monks in various locations on the edge of the desert in Lower Egypt. What marked him
out as different from his contemporaries and predecessors was his
willingness to penetrate the 'inner desert'; in other words, to cut
himself off from all human contact for years at a time. For Anthony,
at least in Athanasius' telling of his story, the job of the monk was
to confront the Devil and his attendant demons. This might be
done anywhere, but one was more likely to encounter the Devil by
drawing attention to oneself, and this Anthony did by inhabiting
tomb chambers and deserted fortresses alone and in the desert.
Anthony's solitude made it impossible for him to secure help from
any human agency; he was reliant only on his own faith and inner
strength. The torments described by Athanasius read to us today
like inner psychological conflicts: visions of horrible creatures,
the fear of being alone in the desert, uncertainty whether he had
sufficient food to survive. To Athanasius' readers, the appearance
of demons or other creatures in dreams was normal; indeed, it
was a mark of spiritual distinction to be subject to such visitations.
Only special people with special powers tended to have visions:
Constantine's vision at Milvian Bridge was the other side of the
coin of Anthony's demons.

Anthony's ability to withstand the assaults of the Devil on his mental stability proved him as a monk. He attracted disciples, just as he himself had sought out more expert monks in his youth, and much of Athanasius' biography consists of advice and spiritual encouragement given by Anthony for his followers. In Anthony's life we see for the first time a pattern that will be repeated in countless biographical studies of solitary monks from the fourth to fourteenth centuries: spiritual power conferred by the successful endurance of solitude.

In contrast to this model of solitude was the communal or cenobitic life. The word 'cenobitic' derives from the Greek *koinobion*, meaning literally a 'communal group'. Although the origins of cenobitic monasticism are traditionally ascribed to a former Roman soldier, Pachomios, he was not the first to initiate or foster this monastic model. At around the same time as the Hellenized Egyptian Pachomios was founding his monastery of Tabennesi by the Nile in Upper Egypt, the Coptic-speaking Shenoute was also founding his White Monastery in the same region. Both developed similar patterns for communal monasticism independently of one another. Their monasteries were based on discipline and organization. They were huge enterprises, in some ways the agribusinesses of the late Roman world. Their monks were required to work as well as pray. The monks, who numbered several hundred, were divided into teams who alternated their activities so that while some were working in the fields, growing the food needed to sustain the community, others were working in the bakery (every monastery had one, which contained the only oven on the premises) or at craftwork such as basket- or mat-weaving. The daily regimen was interrupted by regular offices of prayers and psalms. The whole principle of Egyptian cenobitic monasticism was to create fixed settlements in the desert. If Anthony took on the Devil by himself, Pachomius and Shenoute wanted to populate the desert with armies of monks who could manage to do together what a single monk might find to be beyond his capacities. The *Life of Anthony* talked about Anthony and his followers making the desert into a city, but whereas individual monks or small groups of monks moving around the desert from one place to another were vulnerable, the cenobitic monasteries provided fixed spiritual fortresses against the Devil. In order to understand the force of this image, we need to remember that Christianity in the Roman Empire was essentially an urban phenomenon. The countryside, wilderness and desert were either empty or still largely pagan in the fourth century. Christians who settled in such areas were therefore missionaries for the new religion.

Thus, by the end of the fourth century, Egypt had two quite different forms of monastic life. The solitude or near-solitude represented in Athanasius' *Life of Anthony* had developed in Lower Egypt into a kind of loose federation of hermitages known as Skete, where monasticism was regulated by custom and example. In contrast, the large monasteries were highly regulated by rules written by their founders, and discipline was preserved by close oversight of the monks.

Palestine
Although later tradition tended to see Egypt as the birthplace of monastic life, in fact there is not much evidence that it began there earlier than in Palestine. Constantine's conversion to Christianity brought in its wake a substantial programme of new building in the Roman province in which the favoured religion had been born. In the 320s, Constantine began building the Anastasis Church (now better known as the Church of the Holy Sepulchre), to commemorate the place of the crucifixion and burial of Christ, the locations of which had supposedly been entrusted to his mother, Helena, in a dream. Soon afterwards churches were built on the site of Jesus' birth at Bethlehem, and at other places in Galilee and Judaea associated with the life of Jesus. During the fourth century, the new religion was mapped out by church-building the length and breadth of the province. The consequence of this was the birth of a new kind of Christian devotion: pilgrimage. Christians from all over the Roman world wanted to see the places where Jesus had preached, performed miracles and suffered. By

the 380s, large parties of Christians were travelling together in groups with their priests from their home parishes, just as today. Egeria, a wealthy Roman woman from Spain, left a vivid account of her pilgrimage in 384. One of the most striking features of her journey around the Holy Land – as it came to be known at around this time – is the role played by monks in facilitating pilgrimage. Already by the 380s, permanent groups of monks were based in Jerusalem and Bethlehem, the centres of pilgrimage; moreover, Egeria encountered solitary and cenobitic monks at many of the sites that she and her fellow pilgrims visited. Monks led the prayers and psalm-singing at each holy place, and reminded the pilgrims of the significance in the Bible of the place where they had stopped. Monasteries that have been excavated in Palestine often show a distinctive feature – the guesthouse, or *xenodochion*, designed to provide shelter and food for pilgrims on their way from one holy place to another. This function was necessary because most Palestinian monasteries were founded in deserted wildernesses away from human habitation. Unlike Egypt, Palestine did not have huge expanses of desert in which it was simply impossible to live without regular supplies of food being brought in from outside. The region to the east and south of Jerusalem (the so-called 'Judaean desert'), however, is semi-desert, in which it is possible to find wilderness within a day's walk of the city itself. The combination of wilderness and the presence of the holy was irresistible. Monks could develop the same kind of 'desert spirituality' based on ascetic virtue as Anthony had in Egypt, but at the same time they could take advantage of an added ingredient. Athanasius, in writing the *Life of Anthony*, had compared his hero to characters in Scripture. Chief among these was the Old Testament prophet Elijah, who was celebrated for having heard the message of God in the wilderness. Anthony, then, was seen as a kind of latter-day Elijah, whose moral authority, like that of the prophet, came from his ability to block out everything else but God's voice in the wilderness. Monks in Palestine, therefore, were not only following the example of Elijah, or for that matter John the Baptist, they were doing so in the very places where the biblical prophets had lived.

Palestine began to attract ascetic-minded Christians from around the eastern Mediterranean from at least the 320s. The first to exploit the potential of the Judaean desert was a monk named Chariton, from Asia Minor. Chariton founded a new kind of monastery and a new kind of monastic life in Palestine: the laura. *Laura* in Greek means 'way' or 'path', and it can refer both to the spiritual path taken by those who followed this way of life, and literally to the path that seems to have been a feature of this kind of monastery. The laura was a perfect way to adapt to the topography of the Judaean desert. The region is split by series of 'wadis' or deep valleys running west to east into the Dead Sea, the lowest point on the planet. Lauras were founded in these wadis, using caves in the rock faces as the monks' cells. Typically monks lived alone or in pairs in these cells for five days at a time, then all the monks joined together for weekend services held in common in the laura's oratory. This meant that although the monks had to provide for themselves, the laura also had an identity as an institution with central buildings such as the church and bakery. Supplies also had to be held in common. The laura was, essentially, a combination of solitary and cenobitic features, and it was distinctive to Palestine. Chariton's longest lasting laura, Souka, was far to the south of Jerusalem, virtually on the edge of the habitable region of the Judaean desert. This community continued in existence well into the Middle Ages, and was only finally abandoned in the mid-thirteenth century.

Chariton may have been the pioneer of the laura, but he was followed, and indeed surpassed as a founder, by another native of Asia Minor, Sabas the Great. Already trained as a monk in his home province, Sabas wandered to the Holy Land in search of a unique kind of monastic life that could be pursued in the shadow of the holy places. He approached another famous laura-founder, Euthymius, to ask if he could join him in the desert, but was told that because of his youth he would first have to be tested further in a cenobitic monastery. Eventually his assiduousness paid off and he was allowed not only to live in Euthymius' laura, to the east of

Jerusalem, but also to accompany the great monastic elder on his solitary wanderings around the Dead Sea during Lent. In the 480s Sabas decided to strike out on his own and founded a new laura that still bears his name: Mar Sabas, in the wadi Kidron, south-east of Bethlehem. Sabas' fame rests on his capacities of organization. He founded several other lauras in the desert, and was given the title 'archimandrite', or head of all the monks in the Judaean desert, by the patriarch of Jerusalem. Like Anthony in Egypt, his reputation for personal monastic virtue opened other doors. Just as Anthony was asked to preach against followers of the heretical teacher Arius in Alexandria in the fourth century, so Sabas was summoned to Jerusalem in the early sixth century to uphold orthodoxy in the face of rival doctrines about the person of Christ. Thanks largely to the force of his personality and his clarity of thought, the Church of Jerusalem remained Orthodox in doctrine in the sixth century when the neighbouring provinces, Egypt and Syria, were torn apart by theological disputes that eventually led to the break-up of the Church.

Syria and Asia Minor

The desert topography of Syria was similar to that of Palestine, and monasticism also appeared here in the fourth century – but with some important differences. In Syria, monks took asceticism to greater lengths than anywhere else in the Mediterranean. Feats of bodily mortification were standard features of their monastic regime. Some monks hung heavy chains around their necks so that they were constantly bent under their weight; others strapped bands or knotted ropes around their chests to constrict their breathing; in some monasteries, the presence of niches cut into walls testifies to the practice of standing for hours in one place without being able to move; in others, monks apparently stood on poles all night in vigils of prayer. The most incredible such feat is the practice of monks being suspended all night from the ceiling in a standing position by means of ropes looped under their arms. Nowhere else did monks invent such strange and harsh forms of self-denial to prove their devotion to the monastic ideal.

The most important early example of Syrian monastic asceticism was Jacob of Nisibis (d.388). A solitary monk, he lived out of doors in the mountains outside Nisibis in Mesopotamia, resorting to a cave only in the severe winter weather, eating only uncooked food and scorning clothes altogether. The real star in the Syrian ascetic firmament, however, was a fifth-century monk called Symeon, who invented a whole new concept in asceticism, by which he is still known: the stylite. Symeon was born in c.386 in north Syria into a Christian family. He left home while still young to become a monk, but his experiences in two cenobitic monasteries, Tel'ada and Telneshe, were unrewarding and led to suspicion and distrust on the part of his superiors. In fact, Symeon was asked to leave by one abbot when he refused to tone down his severe ascetic practices, lest he set examples to the other monks that they were unable to follow and which might prove dangerous to them. Symeon settled in a cave for a while, but in c.412 he hit upon the idea of a pillar as the ideal place in which to live an ascetic life. In all he lived on three pillars, each higher than the last, spending the last forty years of his life (he died in 459) about 60 feet off the ground. His pillar had a platform six feet square on top, and railings all around to prevent him from falling to his death. Food was winched up to him in a basket, and not surprisingly, the novelty of his chosen style of asceticism soon attracted attention. By the time he died, he was known as far afield as Britain, and had been consulted by emperors as well as by the local peasantry. Symeon understood that to be ascetic was only half the story; one also had to be seen to be ascetic. Dependent as he was on local society for his food, he provided, in return, the service of visible holiness for the local community. He was, in a way, a kind of mascot or charm, whose constant sacrifice guaranteed luck and divine favour.

Why was this kind of extreme asceticism so rampant in Syria? One possible answer is the topography and geography. Unlike Egypt, where the desert was the land beyond civilization, the Syrian wilderness was habitable, and villages lay scattered around its edges. This meant that it was possible to occupy the desert while still living within the range of human habitation, and thus to be visible in a way that Anthony could only be to others who penetrated the inner desert. Historically, Syria also offered a different past from Egypt and Palestine. Perhaps because of its location as a crossroads between the Roman and Persian empires, the persecution of Christians in the late third and early fourth centuries had never reached the heights that it had in Asia Minor or Egypt. But during the fourth century the Persians began to threaten the eastern frontiers, with the result that Christian communities in Syria were attacked. This meant that the relationship between monasticism and martyrdom was quite different: rather than providing a substitute for martyrdom which was no longer possible, in Syria monasticism might itself prove to be a route to martyrdom. Whereas in Egypt, Palestine and elsewhere in the Empire, self-denial on the part of the monk was an attempt to recreate the self-sacrifice of the martyrs, in fourth-century Syria self-denial and the risk of martyrdom went hand-in-hand.

By the beginning of the fifth century, monastic life everywhere in the eastern Mediterranean was becoming subject to regulation. Most of this was self-imposed, in the sense that founders composed rules for their communities, though imperial laws from the sixth century onward also show the close interest of the government in ensuring both that monasteries were protected and that monks and nuns conformed to their founders' rules. However, there were no clear rules governing who might establish a monastery or under what conditions. The commonest form of foundation probably took the form of a group of ascetic-minded followers gathering around a solitary monk, such as happened with Sabas in the wadi Kidron. However, other foundations may have been even more spontaneous. The great patriarch of Constantinople John Chrysostom (literally, 'golden-mouthed' – a tribute to his eloquence), delivered a series of homilies while still a priest in Antioch in the 370s about the monks who had settled in the mountains around the city. He describes a community that had developed its own liturgical forms and way of life based on observing strict bodily asceticism – in contrast, as he pointed out, to the lives of dissipation being led in the city. If these monks had a founder, his name has long been lost to posterity, and it is more likely that the community emerged without any particular leadership.

Any family or individual could found a monastic community on private land. This is what seems to have happened in a number of cases in Asia Minor. Monasticism here emerged toward the end of the fourth century, under the influence of a particular group of landowners in Cappadocia. The guiding light behind it was Basil of Caesarea. Born into a prominent landowning family, Basil was educated according to the traditional classical syllabus in Constantinople. Before becoming bishop of his home town, Basil travelled through Palestine and into Egypt to study the example of ascetics in the Judaean desert and Skete. His own form of monasticism, however, was to be quite different from anything he had seen before. Basil persuaded his sister, Macrina, who was already committed to the unmarried life of an ascetic virgin, to live in retirement on one of the family estates with a like-minded community. He wrote a series of rules for them that, because of its deeply reflective qualities, came to be the nearest thing in Orthodox Christianity to a standard monastic rule. Basil's 'country-house' monasticism laid stress not so much on mortification of the body as on mental discipline, quiet study and routine. The relationship between the superior and the monks, the need for constant guidance in the path of virtue, the virtue of work and reflection – these were the keynotes of Basil's monasticism. In the wooded glades of Cappadocia, deep in what had become the heartland of rural Christian society, asceticism took on a moderate cast.

The West

Early monasticism was both local and international. Monks, whether solitary or cenobitic, developed their ascetic regimes and their habitats according to local custom. Living in a cave, for example, made sense as a means of secluding oneself in a habitat where there were plenty of such natural features in the landscape. But monks also learned from each other, through travel and an extensive network of contacts between different groups. Just as Chariton, Euthymius and Sabas were drawn to Palestine because of the attraction of the holy city, so Evagrius Pontus and John Cassian were drawn to Egypt because of the fame of the 'desert fathers' who had turned the deserts into cities of ascetics.

Cassian, unlike the monastic founders we have encountered so far, was a Latin speaker from the western half of the Empire. Having begun his monastic career in a communal monastery in Bethlehem in the late fourth century, he left to study what he thought were the sources of ascetic life in Egypt. By his own account he wandered throughout Skete, in the western desert near Alexandria, and also visited another concentration of hermit-monks at Nitria, to learn the precepts of asceticism. In the early fifth century he went back to the west and settled in the more amenable climate of southern France to found his own monastery on the isle of Lérins.

Simultaneously, however, a native monastic tradition was emerging in Gaul, Italy and North Africa, under the guidance of bishops such as Martin of Tours and Augustine of Hippo. This was of a very different order from the ascetic extremes encountered in Egypt or Syria. Augustine's idea of monastic life, for example, was simply for the clergy of his city to live communally and in celibacy, rather than marrying and living among their flock. The western half of the Roman Empire – Gaul, Spain, Italy, North Africa and Britain – was far more rural than the urbanized east. Here, the leadership of the Church fell into the hands of the traditional aristocracy, as the landowners exchanged the robes of senators and magistrates for the bishop's pallium. Christianity had grown fastest in the cities of the Empire, and by the end of the fifth century there were still significant areas of the countryside where the old religions, based on local pre-Roman deities, were still worshipped. Monasticism was a tool in the armoury of bishops like Martin, who were trying to replace a kaleidoscope of such traditions with the universal religion of Christ.

Another strand in the fabric of monasticism in the West was provided by the social hierarchy. The western provinces were lost to the imperial government during the fifth century. The Empire in the West did not 'fall' as such; rather it changed out of all recognition over the course of three or four generations, as government and military affairs in Gaul, Spain, Britain and even Italy came to be dominated by Germanic peoples – primarily the Goths, Franks and Burgundians. Roman *society* did not end; indeed, the new ruling classes were already highly Romanized and wished to profit from Roman government rather than put an end to it. But political change meant that the old senatorial aristocracy was disenfranchised. Most retired to their estates to cultivate and preserve what they could of their culture. Because most of them were Christian by c.AD 500, this meant they were laying the foundations for the synthesis of classical culture and Christian teaching that would dominate western civilization for centuries. A striking example of this phenomenon is the community at Vivarium, in southern Italy, founded by Cassiodorus in the early sixth century. An aristocrat of senatorial rank, Cassiodorus had been the chief minister of the Gothic king of Italy, Theodoric. When his master died in 526, Cassiodorus retired to a country villa which he filled with a library and like-minded men of culture in search of peace and quiet. Although its primary purpose was the pursuit of leisure for the study of classical learning, Vivarium functioned as a kind of monastery for intellectuals, in which a measured and temperate life was taken as axiomatic.

By the middle of the sixth century, a number of variant traditions of monastic living were current in the western provinces. At this stage, although it had begun to be divided into separate Germanic kingdoms, the West had not yet lost touch with the eastern Empire. Cassiodorus, for example, probably knew the works of Basil in Greek as well as in Latin translations. Anyone wishing to become a monk could choose between a number of styles of ascetic living, or even invent his or her own. What was lacking was a definitive formula that could consciously unite the best in these traditions into a synthesis. That was left to the most famous monastic figure in the West, often seen as the father of Catholic monasticism: St Benedict of Nursia.

Nothing is really known about Benedict's life other than what is told in the *Dialogues* of Gregory the Great, which was written a couple of generations after Benedict. From this source, which is far from reliable as an historical text, we can reconstruct something of his career. Benedict seems to have begun his ascetic life as a solitary hermit in central Italy, probably in the middle decades of the sixth century. This was a period of profound political and economic turmoil in Italy, as the Gothic successors of Theodoric fought to hold on to the kingdom he had founded against attempts by the eastern emperor, Justinian, to reconquer lost western provinces. As always, prolonged war meant that the civilian population suffered; probably in these circumstances, many people, not just monks, fled into mountains and hills. Benedict seems to have established a reputation as a holy man and attracted the attention of a group of monks who wanted to found a cenobitic community. They asked him to be their superior. He refused, preferring a life of solitude; they pressed him, and eventually he was persuaded to undertake the task, with the warning that they would not necessarily like the life he proposed they should lead.

If the *Dialogues* present a semi-legendary monastic founder, the *Rule of Benedict*, which was probably composed in the 560s, offers a humane and wise blend of existing monastic traditions. Benedict's *Rule* is essentially a practical document. It was designed for the express purpose of governing a cenobitic community. Where it differs from the monastic legislation of his predecessors such as Pachomios, Sabas or even Basil, is that it was not intended simply for a *specific* community but for any monastic community. The *Rule* includes specific detailed instructions covering the internal running of the monastery, down to the amount of food to be provided, the nature of the monks' clothing and even the books they should read. But Benedict also inserted spiritual reflections on humility, the relationship between the superior and his flock, and the role of the monk in the community. The intention was to provide a blue-print for what Benedict saw as the principles of the monastic life.

Naturally, Benedict borrowed from previous monastic writers, especially John Cassian and Basil. But he also made clear his own views on the superiority of cenobitic monasticism over all other forms, and he was particularly scathing about what he called *gyrovagi* (literally, 'people who wander in circles'). He had no time for solitaries who wandered about from one monastery or settle-ment to another in the expectation of spending indefinite amounts of time in different communities as the whim took them. Nor did he respect monks who lived in small unstructured groups without definite leadership or regulation. Benedict refers to the monastery as a school in which the precepts of ascetic living must be learned. Monasticism, in his view, was a gradual process of attaining self-awareness, with the eventual goal of total absorption of oneself in God. The monastic day was to be divided into three sets of activities: prayer, meaning liturgical observance in church; work, which might be any form of manual labour; and sleep. The day was divided, however, so that both sleep and work were interrupted by regular 'hours', or liturgical offices, at set points during the 24-hour period. The earliest monasteries whose liturgical observances are known to us probably had only two such offices daily, but already by the turn of the sixth century as many as six or seven seem to have been standard in Syria. In contrast to Syrian ascetic excesses, however, Benedict advocated a relatively mild regime of discip-line. In keeping with his idea of the monastery as a school, and monastic life as progression, he warned against extremes of self-mortification, and left a great deal to the abbot's discretion. Above all, the abbot was to be – as indeed the name *abba* suggests – the father of the monks, his relationship with them mirroring that of God to his people.

SOURCES OF EVIDENCE: HOW DO WE KNOW?

Most of what we know about early monasticism comes from a smallish group of texts initially written in Greek, some of which were then translated into other languages in use in different regions of the Near East, or on which different versions in other languages were subsequently based. Athanasius, bishop of Alexandria (296–373), deserves the title of the first author to write specifically about Christian monasticism. His *Life of Anthony* was written in c.357 and first translated into Latin for a western Mediterranean audience in the 360s. A second translation followed in 370, and in 376 Jerome wrote a *Life of Paul of Thebes* that, although now regarded as having been about an invented rather than a real monk, was heavily influenced by Athanasius' work. The extent of this influence can be seen in the effect that the *Life of Anthony* supposedly had on Augustine, who later attributed his conversion to Christianity in 386 to being inspired by hearing the story of Anthony.

The idea of writing a biography of a holy man was not in itself exclusive to Christianity – the third-century pagan Neoplatonist Plotinus had found an admiring biographer in his pupil Porphyry – but Athanasius was certainly also influenced by the tradition of Christian martyrdom about which his older contemporaries such as Eusebius and Lactantius had already written. However, the *Life of Anthony* is much more than simply a biography. Anthony's life posed problems for a biographer because for long periods he did not actually *do* anything – or, rather, what he did was contemplative rather than active, and therefore defied description. Athanasius' biography is thus in many ways an intellectual study rather than a 'life story', and although the outlines of Anthony's long life do emerge, Athanasius' chief concern is to give a portrait of monastic spirituality. Thus, many chapters are devoted to Anthony's advice to other monks and to descriptions of the fantastic and terrifying visions of demons that he experienced in his solitude. For Athanasius, the inner man was more important than the details of how or where Anthony lived, and although he locates the biography in the physical geography of the Egyptian desert, it was the mental geography of Anthony's journey towards God that really interested him, and that proved so influential.

One of the reasons why we can be sure that Anthony was in fact an historical figure rather than simply an invention on the part of Athanasius is that other traditions about him survive in other sources. One of these is an anecdotal collection of little pen-portraits of Egyptian monks known as the *Apophthegmata Patrum*, or *Sayings of the Fathers*. One historian has described the inhabitants of the collection as 'a motley band of colourful characters, wild adventures, and stinging, memorable "one-liners"'.[2] This is the authentic voice of the Egyptian peasant, rather than of an educated Greek-speaker like Athanasius, and the characters who emerge from the pages of the *Apophthegmata* speak with folk wisdom rather than theological learning. For this reason, details of everyday life as it was lived by the monks flash vividly before us even today – what the monks ate and wore, their living spaces and, above all, their conversation provide the materials of their simple but powerful spirituality. Although the *Apophthegmata* was first written down in Greek, and in fifth-century Palestine rather than Egypt, it certainly reflects an older Coptic oral tradition. But the *Apophthegmata* proved so influential that similar collections were made in Syriac, Coptic, Armenian, Georgian, Arabic and Ethiopic – languages that describe a geographical arc around the monastic landscape of the Near East.

By AD 400, monasticism in Lower Egypt was already so well established that many of the monks had settled there from other parts of the Roman world. One of these, Palladius, was born in Asia Minor in 363, but had been both a monk in the Holy Land and a student in Alexandria before joining the monks at Nitria and then Kellia. Much later, in the 420s, after a career that included becoming a bishop in his homeland followed by political exile in Upper Egypt for his support for the disgraced bishop of Constantinople, John Chrysostom, he wrote his *Lausiac History*, a memoir of his Egyptian experiences. The *Lausiac History*, like the *Apophthegmata*, takes the form of pen-portraits – about 70 in all – but unlike the *Apopthegmata*, Palladius' work reflects his theological training. The monks and their stories are vehicles for Palladius to share his concerns about the meaning of monasticism within the Christian life and Christian theology. An anonymous work similarly based on individual monastic portraits, the *History of the Monks of Egypt* is an account of a journey made by seven Palestinian monks from Lycopolis, in the Thebaid in Upper Egpyt, to the monastic colonies of Nitria and Kellia in Lower Egypt and ultimately to Diolcos on the Mediterranean coast. Although some of the characters are the same as those about whom Palladius would also write, the author of the *History of the Monks* was more interested in the exotic and the miraculous – a sign that Egyptian monasticism was already, at the beginning of the fifth century, regarded as a phenomenon apart.

The format of Palladius' *Lausiac History* provided a template for three important writers who wanted to promote the claims for monastic holiness in their own regions of the Mediterranean world. In the fifth century, a Syrian bishop, Theodoret of Cyrrhus (c.393–c.457), recorded the exploits of monks and hermits of his region of northern Syria, including the first account of the remarkable Symeon the Stylite, in his *Religious History*. Subsequently, the distinctive quality of Syrian asceticism was given further exposure by the sixth-century bishop John of Ephesus, whose collection of biographies of Syrian monks reflects the divisions that had ruptured the Church by the time he was writing. The wider context of monasticism for John was not, as it had been for Athanasius, a polemical struggle against paganism, but the defence of Syrian Monophysite theology against the mainstream. In sixth-century Palestine, Cyril of Scythopolis based his collection of monastic biographies on the dominant figure of Sabas, the founder and organizer of lauras in the Judean desert. Where the Syrian monks provide awe-inspiring examples of self-mortification through the terrifying solitude and horrific deprivation some monks imposed on themselves, the picture provided by Cyril is quieter and gentler. There are fewer instances of genuinely heroic asceticism of the kind that it would be difficult for us to imagine enduring; instead, Cyril shows us small communities of monastic leaders and their disciples following a simple life of prayer and contemplation governed by gentle rhythms of alternating solitude and communal worship.

In retrospect, the period between Athanasius' *Life of Anthony* and the spread of the Arabs with their new monotheistic religion of Islam looked like a golden age. Between the fourth and seventh centuries, monasticism provided the spiritual currency of the whole of the region dominated by the Mediterranean. Monks could find, amid different customs and liturgical observances, familiar elements of their way of life from the Atlantic to the Dead Sea. The coming of the Arabs and Islam did not put an end to monasticism, but it finished the monastic commonwealth in which seekers after a holy life could wander almost at will throughout the Empire. The last such monk was John Moschus. Born in Damascus in c.550, John became a monk at the monastery of St Theodosius near Bethlehem, and lived for a while at Sabas' laura in the Kidron Valley, before moving to Sinai and then, in the early years of the seventh century, settling in Egypt and later living for a while in Cyprus. He died in Rome in 619. A year earlier, the Persian invasion of Palestine destroyed many of the monasteries in the region where he had begun his spiritual journey; thirty years later, Syria, Palestine and Egypt had been annexed by the Arabs and cut off from the Roman Empire. John's *Spiritual Meadow*, rather like an Edwardian novel, provides a glimpse of a world before it vanished forever.

*   *   *

A fundamental question is raised implicitly by all these sources: How far can they be trusted? When, for example, Palladius tells us in the *Lausiac History* that the monk Heron used to survive for periods of three months on only wild lettuce and the eucharist, then eat sparingly for another three months, then fast again for the next three, is this to be taken literally? Likewise, did Athanasius really mean that Anthony lived only off bread and salt while he was holed up in an abandoned fortress in the desert? Are we really to believe that Onuphrios, the solitary monk in the Sinai peninsula, lived solely off the dates that fell, twelve large bunches a year, from his date palm? And even if he had been able to put up with the tedium of this diet, could he have sustained life on it?[3]

These are the fundamental questions that historians have to resolve whatever the source or period they are studying. Contemporary accounts have to be understood not as objective reports of 'what actually happened', but as opinions and commentaries by observers on 'what was going on'. It is an important distinction, for it allows the observer licence to exaggerate, misrepresent, or use facts selectively in order to get across a picture of people and events that may in general be quite accurate. A given account may be more concerned with establishing patterns of ideal behaviour than with historical facts. As Leontius of Naples expressed it in his *Life of Symeon the Holy Fool*, the purpose of his writing was to 'unveil . . . a nourishment that does not die but that leads our souls to eternal life.'[4] Perhaps Onuphrios lived *principally* off dates, supplemented by food brought to him by visiting monks; or perhaps the period he fasted in this way was much shorter than the whole span of his adult life that we are supposed to believe. The point being made, imaginatively, is that he was a genuine ascetic, a holy man. Stories that play on exaggerations of basic truths about people are a way of making this point. Some of the literature is intended to be for instruction, some ethical or moral, and some to furnish historical accounts of how monasticism, especially in the eastern Mediterranean, began and how it worked in practice. Some of it, too, has a polemical agenda. A writer who wanted to emphasize the holiness of a given monk would naturally dwell on austerity as one of the factors making up that special quality. Conversely, a monk who was regarded as having 'failed' in other ways could naturally not be found to have succeeded in proper asceticism as regards eating.

Most historians take it for granted that the body of material assembled in the instructional literature should not be taken literally in all its details, that it is intended to give an impression of ideals rather than to convey facts. I shall return to the question of Onuphrios' dates further on in the book. Just as we cannot assume that the author of the story was using rhetorical licence, nor can we reject such details out of hand. We may, for example, be sceptical about the practice attributed in an anonymous text known as the *Paradise of the Fathers* to Abba Isaiah, who allegedly used to take the saucepan off the fire just as the lentils were starting to boil, saying that just to see the fire cooking the food was sustenance enough. But the practice of eating partly-boiled pulses is attested elsewhere, for example in Jerome's *Life of Hilarion*, where Hilarion is said to have eaten semi-cooked lentils for three years during his twenties as part of his abstinence. Was Jerome also exaggerating? He cannot have been copying the practice from the *Paradise of the Fathers,* for that was written many years later and in Syriac, a language unknown to him. It is more likely that the practice was a well-known trope by the time the anonymous author of the *Paradise* used it for Isaiah. If Jerome was the inventor of the trope, he did at least give it some verisimilitude by observing that in his final years Hilarion was so troubled by digestive problems that he could only manage thin broth – doubtless, the effect of the uncooked lentils of his youth.

If such details of asceticism and self-denial are inventions or exaggerations, they not only follow an internal logic, but also offer a set of symbols, rather like a code, which can be understood and picked up by other writers. We will see examples of this later on in the book, when we encounter particular traits or details of ascetic practices that appear to have been repeated across centuries in widely different contexts. Thus, when we read that Bernard of Clairvaux, a twelfth-century monk noted for his personal austerity of living, also suffered from digestive problems later in life, we cannot be sure whether this is a plausible statement of fact on the part of his biographer, or a coded clue designed to alert the reader to the same detail in Jerome's *Life of Hilarion*. For such a system of allusions and clues to work, of course, writers had to rely on a certain set of knowledge on the part of their readers. The clue would have no purpose if Bernard's biographer had not thought it likely that his readers would also be familiar with Jerome's work. As it happens, we know from catalogues of medieval libraries, as well as from extensive quotation by many monastic authors, that Jerome's works, including the *Life of Hilarion*, were widely read in twelfth-century monasteries. A monk reading the biography of Bernard would thus, in all likelihood, make the intended connection between Bernard and the early Christian ascetic. Once made in the mind of a reader, such a connection, although made in the context of food and diet, would not necessarily be restricted to that subject. For if Bernard was thought of in connection with Jerome, or even as a Jerome-like character, in that respect, why not also in others?

We also need to bear in mind that examples of extreme asceticism cannot be taken as blanket descriptions of how *all* early Christian monks or their medieval imitators lived. This was not the purpose of authors of such accounts – for one thing, if all monks and nuns had lived such austere lives, there would be little point in singling out some for special remark. If some sources suggest that monks were almost superhuman in their capacity for personal austerity when it came to food, others indicate that quite a wide variety of foods was eaten in monasteries and by solitaries. These include beans, lentils, cabbage, olives, fish, oil, leeks and onions, garlic, cheese, buffalo milk, berries, figs, nuts, radishes, carob and a whole category of herbs and plants harvested in the wild. This book will explore some of these foods, suggest how they might have been used, and examine the part played by growing, cultivating and harvesting foods in the lives of monks and hermits. It also offers suggestions for some of the apparently less plausible foods eaten by hermits.

Chapter Two

Desert fathers, pillar-saints and fasting

Eat grass, wear grass and sleep on grass,
and your heart will become like iron.

GRAZING

We have already met in passing Onuphrios and his dates, Anthony and his bread and salt, Heron's wild-lettuce diet, and Hilarion and his half-cooked lentils. Jerome, in his *Life of Hilarion*, was very precise about the kinds and quantities of food the hermit supposedly ate. Between the ages of 20 and 26, for the first three years, he ate a daily ration of lentils soaked in cold water but uncooked, followed by a further three years on bread, salt and water. There then followed three more years on wild herbs and roots that he gathered himself. From 30 to 35, he rationed himself to six ounces of barley bread daily, accompanied by a portion of lightly-cooked vegetables, eaten without oil. He seems to have settled on this diet for most of the rest of his life, though after the age of thirty-five he added a dressing of olive oil to the vegetables for the sake of his health. Then, after the age of sixty-three, when his digestion began to protest at his youthful austerities, he was reduced to a broth of herbs and meal, which he took once daily, at sunset. Hilarion's diet may not have been typical, in the sense that it lacked variety and the quantities were very small, but the foods he ate – stewed vegetables, pulses and bread – formed, with fruit in season, the staples of monastic food in the Near East.[1]

There are plenty of individual examples of austerity regarding

Hawthorn Porridge

Gather as many hawthorn blossoms as you can; ideally, you should have about two handfuls for a good hermit's serving. Crush the petals in a mortar until you have a thickish paste. In a small saucepan, gently heat half a pint of milk, and stir in the hawthorn paste. Tear or grate two slices of stale bread into pieces, and stir gently into the milk. Let it cook until the bread has amalgamated with the milk to thicken it to a porridge-like consistency.

eating and drinking in the sources mentioned in the previous chapter. Dioscorus, one of the monks of Skete encountered in the *Sayings of the Fathers,* set himself a new ascetic challenge every year: one year he undertook only to eat raw food, another year, not to eat fruit, though he was very fond of it, and so on. Abba Sisoes of Thebes would eat either bread or vegetables, but not both at the same meal. Macarius, the doyen of the Skete monks, copied what he had heard was the practice of the monks of Pachomius' monastery Tabennesi, to eat only raw food in Lent – but he extended this for a period of seven years without a break.[2] He was also frugal about eating fruit. One year he had a yearning for the first grapes from the harvest, but when someone sent a bunch to him he sent them on to another monk rather than give way to his desire. Abba Arsenius, however, ate a tiny quantity of fresh fruit as soon as it ripened on the trees, so as to be able to give thanks to God for the goodness of creation. An unnamed monk in Palladius' *Lausiac History,* who suffered from extreme digestive disorder, was given a dish of stewed prunes to alleviate it. He refused on the grounds that it would break his vow of fasting on bread and water alone (the regime that had doubtless caused the disorder in the first place). An Egyptian monk named Isaiah was visited in the desert of Skete by another monk. He offered him some food and put a saucepan of lentils on the fire, but just as the water was starting to boil, he removed the pan, saying that simply to see the fire cooking the lentils should be sustenance enough for them.[3] There was an element of competition in some of these stories. Macarius was inspired by the example of a monk who ate only a pound of bread a day to break up his own bread ration into pieces and keep it in a jar with a narrow neck; he then ate daily only the pieces that he could bring up in a single handful.[4]

The Syriac translation of the *Lausiac History* tells the story of an Egyptian monk called Paphnutios, who had sworn not to drink wine. Once, when he was living as a solitary, he was set upon by a band of robbers and tormented by them. Their idea of entertainment at his expense was to force the monk to drink wine, on penalty of death. Eventually, after an internal struggle, Paphnutios reasoned that it was better to forsake his own vow under such compulsion rather than permit his captors to commit the sin of murder.[5]

Theodosius, a Palestinian monk who followed the custom of spending the season of Lent wandering around the Dead Sea in imitation of the example of John the Baptist, scolded a disciple whom he had invited to accompany him one year, when he saw the younger monk bringing a pot and pan with him. If he needed to eat cooked food, Theodosius chastised him, he should go elsewhere. (In fact, it is possible to 'cook' food from its raw state without using fire or a pan, though an earthenware pot is needed.) Another Skete monk, Isaiah, was criticized for adding water and salt to his food, on the grounds that this created a sauce, which was unnecessarily complicating the basic ingredients. Aphrodisias, a monk at the monastery founded by Theodosius, imposed a penance on himself for once having killed a mule in a blind rage. From that time on, he would only eat the leftovers of the other monks' food, which he mixed together in a single bowl, and of which he permitted himself to eat just a little each day. When the leftovers kept in this way began to smell or when he noticed that worms were breeding in it, he just added fresh leftovers to the bowl. He kept up this practice for some thirty years without ever falling ill or suffering from digestive complaints. Other people's leftovers, of course, will always appear less appetising than uneaten food one has prepared oneself. The lesson of thrift was well taught by Sabas in the Great Laura. On one occasion he noticed James, the monk whose turn it was to cook for the guesthouse, throwing out into the wadi the leftovers of the communal dish of bean stew. Sabas, without saying anything to James, went secretly into the wadi, picked up the beans and spread them out on to the rocks to dry. Much later, when it was his turn to do kitchen duty in the guesthouse, Sabas invited James to dine there, and served up the same beans, recooked in a stew. James declared than he had never tasted a better dish, whereupon Sabas revealed where the beans had come from.[6]

Eating raw as opposed to uncooked food was regarded as particularly virtuous by some monks. There were two ethical aspects to the ideal: first, the desire to spend no longer than the absolute minimum on the preparation of food, so as to preserve the state of indifference to it; and second, the belief that food in its original state most closely resembled what Adam and Eve had eaten in the Garden of Eden. Fruit that could simply be picked from trees was perfect – though Sabas renounced apples, which he loved, in memory of the fruit that had first caused humans to sin. There is, perhaps, a distant spiritual echo in this belief of a contemporary concern for 'low-impact' living – the closer to its original source and state the food, the better it is, both nutritionally and in environmental terms.

But gathering and eating food from the wild was also a necessity for some solitaries, especially if they chose to settle in areas where there was no settled habitation. Eating wild plants and roots may sometimes have been a necessity, but it developed into a recognizable part of monastic tradition. A category of monk known as *boschoi* (literally, 'grazers') features prominently in early Byzantine literature. The earliest reference is probably in a fourth-century sermon by Ephrem the Syrian, which speaks of desert fathers living rough in the Syrian mountains, wearing sackcloth and grazing off the land like deer. The whole earth and all the mountains, Ephrem proclaimed, are their table, for they eat simply

Hermit's stew

Collect a large bunch of mixed leaves and shoots of various kinds: for example, dandelion, wild asparagus, alexanders, wild chervil, nettles. Clean carefully and trim off excess stalks. You should end up with shoots and leaves about 4 inches in length. Heat some olive oil in a wide-bottomed saucepan and add a finely chopped onion. When this is translucent, throw in your herbs and mix them around until they are coated with the oil. Then add about half a pint of water and a tablespoon of mild vinegar; *bon viveurs* may prefer to use a mixture of water and white wine. Bring to the boil and simmer. Meanwhile crush two bulbs of garlic and half a small chilli in a mortar. Add a few chopped almonds or pine nuts and a small handful of parsley or coriander. Check that the leaves and shoots in your stew, which will have reduced in volume, are tender. The length of time this will take will vary depending on the quantity and the varieties of leaves in your pot. Add salt and the crushed mixture in your mortar. Eat with flat bread, or thicken with boiled tree bark [see Chapter 3].

what they find growing around them in the wild. Writing in about AD 425, the historian Sozomen mentioned hermits taking sickles up to the mountains so that they could cut themselves plants for food, like animals at pasture. 'These monks of Syria were called *boschoi* when they first embarked on the philosophic life, because they had no dwellings, ate neither bread nor meat, and drank no wine . . . When it was time to eat, each one would take a sickle, go up to the mountains and feed on what grew there, like animals at the pasture.' In the *Life of Symeon the Holy Fool*, which is set in the seventh-century, Symeon answers his companion John's question 'What shall we eat?' before they embark on an anchoritic life, by saying, 'What those who are called the Grazers eat.' They had learned about the way of life from the superior of the monastery of St Gerasimus by the Jordan.[7] Grazing seems to have been primarily a Syrian and Palestinian way of life. This is because in Egypt it simply was not possible to live off what one could find growing wild – one either grew one's own food or, in the desert, survived on dates and bread brought from settled communities. Even Anthony, when he settled in the desert near the Red Sea, brought grain with him and tools to grow his own food. It is true that in *Sayings of the Fathers*, Macarius describes monks who lived with animals in the desert, but he seems to have been talking about bare survival for a limited period rather than a way of life. The text known as the *History of the Monks of Egypt*, written in c.400, says that some of the early solitaries ate herbs and roots, but that before long the norm was for Egyptian monks to grow food. A monk named Apollo was typical of the earlier generation of hermits, eating only plants that 'sprang up naturally from the soil, and eschewing bread, beans and lentils.'[8]

But in the semi-desert of Syria and Palestine it was always possible to find wild roots like melagria, or a variety of edible leaves. Thus, when Euthymius and Theoctistus first settled in a cave in the Judaean desert, they fed off the plants that happened to grow there. Later, in retreat from their coenobium near the Dead Sea, Euthymius resorted once again to eating meloa, a shrubby plant that grows commonly near river banks in the region. Sabas, when he settled in his cave in the wadi Kidron, was joined by other solitaries and grazers, according to Cyril of Scythopolis. Sabas himself recalled living off melagria with Euthymius during Lent. He seems to have adopted the practice from his own mentor, for when he was later found wandering around the shores of the Dead Sea by himself during Lent, his pouch was full of melagria and reed hearts.[9]

Melagria has been identified as *Asphodelus microcarpus*. It is a shrub with tough and inedible leaves, commonly found in the Judaean desert, and indigenous to Syria and Palestine. Although the leaves cannot be eaten, its roots are edible and can be used as a substitute for onions or garlic when boiled or sautéed. Alternatively, gum resin from the roots can be used to flavour dishes of beans or herbs. When Sabas lived in solitude in the Judaean desert, his food bag apparently contained only asphodel and reed hearts, as well as a small trowel used for digging the asphodel out of the ground. Meloa, also known as salt bush, is a form of mallow; its leaves and root are both edible. Cyril of Scythopolis' *Life of Euthymius* describes monks at Euthymius' laura washing meloa leaves that they had gathered, so clearly it was a plant eaten by settled monks as well as grazers. These practices conform in their essentials to those described by Charles Doughty, the nineteenth-century English traveller in Arabia. Doughty, who was indigent and ran out of the supplies he had brought to the desert, learnt from the Beduin how to find and eat wild leeks and wild sorrel in the upland areas of Arabia. He also found small tubers which he described as tasting like potatoes. The deserts of Arabia, Syria and Palestine are in fact surprisingly fertile, with many halophytes (salt-tolerant plants) and xerophytes (drought-resistant) species such as purslane growing there. Although the average annual rainfall in these deserts is low, when they arrive the rains can be remarkably heavy, albeit for short periods. A few days of heavy rainbursts can revive apparently dried-up shrubs and promote sudden growth among seeds latent in the sand.[10]

On another occasion, when forced into exile from the Great Laura, Sabas fed off carobs gathered from a tree. The monk John the Cilician, one of the monks described by Cyril of Scythopolis, claimed that he had come across elders who lived for seventy years by eating grass and dates. John of Lycopolis, the Egyptian desert monk, supposedly lived off fruit alone, and certainly never ate anything that required cooking. Jacob of Nisibis, who lived out in the open for most of the year, retiring to a cave only in the winter, is described by the fifth-century writer Theodoret of Cyrrhus in the following way: 'For food he did not have that which is laboriously sown and reaped, but that which grows of its own accord. He gathered the spontaneous fruits of wild trees and herbs which looked like vegetables, and of these he gave the body the necessities of life, renouncing the use of fire.' As I have remarked, eating raw food was considered to bring one closer to the natural prelapsarian state of humanity. The grazers were clearly extreme examples, even among contemporaries, of a kind of perfection in the monastic life. The observation by Theodoret that Jacob of Nisibis 'renounced the use of fire' indicates this prelapsarian intention on the part of the monk – he wished to live perfectly, as he imagined must have been possible for Adam and Eve in Paradise before the Fall.[11]

The fundamental question we are naturally prompted to ask is, of course, whether it is really possible to survive for periods of more than a few weeks at a time on foraging or grazing in this way. When we read in an early monastic text that monks ate grass, are we to take this literally? Most of us have probably, lazing in a meadow on a summer's day, chewed sweet grass stems, but not for nourishment. Grass was supposedly the staple food of a monk known by John the Cilician, and was recommended in these words by an elderly monk in the *Sayings of the Fathers*: 'Eat grass, wear grass and sleep on grass, and your heart will become like iron.' Is the grass referred to in such texts something different from what we might mean? Most grass has a bitter taste in its raw state, except for the part nearest the root. The stems are also highly indigestible to humans. But we should distinguish between the stems or blades of grass and the seed or grain that grows in high summer. In fact, according to the *U.S. Army Survival Handbook*, there is no wild grass that is known to be harmful to humans. The grains of most grasses can be collected, roasted – or, in hot climates, simply toasted in the sun – or boiled to improve the taste.[12] Even a solitary grazing monk who did not wish to cook could collect grains, spread them on a rock and leave them for several hours for the sun to do its work. He (almost all the grazers known by name were men) might even mix the grains with water to make a dough, without having to infringe the convention against use of fire.

There are many grasses with leaves that are not only edible but are thought to have nutritional value, and a monk who was prepared to cook grass had an even wider field of possibilities. Herbalists have for centuries used couch grass, for example, to make a tea recommended for urinary problems. Foxtail grass, which is found at field margins in western Asia, has been grown as a food crop in parts of Africa; its grains are best eaten boiled. Wheat and barley grass, before they grow their grains, are recognized as having a similar vitamin and mineral make-up to dark-leaf vegetables, although it is the toasted or powdered grain that is most commonly consumed. However, most pertinent to the monks of the Near East is the reed – the plant that, along with melagria, was Sabas' staple diet during his Lenten wanderings. Sabas, evidently something of a connoisseur even in this extreme situation, collected and saved the hearts of the reed. In fact, all parts of the reed, which is a species of grass that can grow up to twelve feet in places, are edible either raw or cooked. The stems are best eaten before they flower in early summer, either boiled or ground into a kind of flour and mixed with water to make a form of bread. Since Sabas took no cooking equipment, he must have simply chewed the raw stems, and saved the hearts. Because his fast occurred in Lent, before the flowering season, he would have been able to enjoy reeds at their best. However, Cyril of Scythopolis also reports an occasion when Sabas was able, through a miracle, to eat raw squills, a plant that is normally considered inedible without cooking.

Cyril of Scythopolis' *Life of Sabas* distinguished between settled and nomadic types of monasticism, the implication being that not all monks are capable of sustaining the practice of grazing, but also that it is a way of life that can be adapted for certain periods, notably during Lent. Some idea of progression toward grazing is given in the sixth-century *Life of Symeon the Holy Fool*, in which Symeon tries, unsuccessfully, to persuade a companion who has just been accepted along with him to the coenobium of Gerasimus to join him in the desert as a grazer instead, without first going through the intermediary stage of laura dwelling. Grazing had a long history in Syrian and Palestinian monasticism. At least fifteen separate grazers, primarily in Judaea, are mentioned in John Moschus' *Spiritual Meadow*. One of the last works of the 'golden age' of early Christian monasticism, the *Spiritual Meadow* has a

Wild grass porridge

Pick as much wild grass as you can find within easy reach. Separate the grain from the stalks, either by hand picking or by beating the heads with a stick. Wash the grains and leave to soak for an hour, then crush in a mortar until you have a fine consistency. Put the grains in a saucepan on medium heat, add water to cover and cook until the grains have absorbed the water but not dried out. For sweet porridge, add honey or sugar; for savoury, salt and pepper, and other flavourings such as chilli, garlic or crushed almonds.

Alternatively, once you have crushed the grains to a fine consistency, you may decide to make hermit's bread instead. Add the grains to some cold water – the exact amount will depend on how much grain you have, but you should aim to produce a firm paste. Mix a little salt into the paste, and then shape into small flat round cakes. If you are in a very hot climate, the traditional hermit's method of cooking these is to leave them in the sun all day until they have hardened, but they can also be cooked in an oven.

nostalgic quality, as John looks for monks carrying on what was already, in the early seventh century, a venerable tradition. In John's day, grazers seem to have travelled in small groups, and to have known one another. Menas, abbot of a coenobium, tells John about the monk Sophronius. 'He grazed around the Dead Sea. For seventy years he went around naked, eating wild plants but nothing else at all.'[13]

Where did the idea of grazing, or living purely off the land as a religious way of life, come from? The earliest writing about monasticism plays up the associations between desert monks and biblical role models. In the Old Testament, pre-eminent among these was the prophet Elijah, but in the early chapters of the New Testament a more spectacular example was provided by John the

Baptist. Everyone knows, or used to know, that John the Baptist lived on locusts and wild honey. Such a diet is not implausible, for both are readily available in the Jordan Valley where he preached. Locusts, along with grasshoppers, crickets, ants and beetles are eaten across the world and relished in many cultures, especially in North America and Asia. Leviticus (11.22) permitted the eating of locusts, bald locusts, beetles and grasshoppers. Locusts and various kinds of grasshoppers are found throughout the world. Although they can be pests for agricultural communities, they have also been harvested as food by native Americans, Africans, Indians and Persians. Herodotus describes the Parthians crushing the locusts into a kind of powder and baking them into small cakes. In Asia they are most commonly eaten today deep fried, sometimes first marinated in soy sauce. Besides, it would have made good sense from a dietary point of view for John the Baptist, or other eremitical monks, to have eaten locusts. There are acknowledged nutritional benefits in eating insects, which provide a remarkably high source of protein. Locusts and grasshoppers contain 40–50 per cent protein in ratio to body mass – which is about three times higher than a beef steak – and also contain calcium, phosphorus, iron and vitamins. Ants, likewise, are widely eaten in Africa. Laurens van der Post, in his memoir of life in the bush in southern Africa, *First Catch your Eland*, recalls how ants used to be called 'bushmen's rice' in the South Africa of his childhood. They are higher in protein per weight than meat or fish – it has been suggested that a 100-gram serving of fried ants or termites contains most of the recommended daily amount of protein for adults.

Travelling in extreme poverty in Arabia with the Beduin in the 1870s, the English adventurer Charles Doughty observed them eating locusts that had first been fried in pits dug in the sand, then seasoned with herbs. They would be preserved in salt and kept in leather bags, then ground and mixed with the sour buttermilk that formed a staple of the Beduin diet. The early spring locusts, however, which are plump from having fed off greenstuff, were considered enough of a delicacy to be eaten whole, simply roasted over the fire.[14]

But were locusts really what John ate? Although the book of Leviticus permits the eating of locusts to the Israelites, there are very few examples of the early Christian hermits, for whom John was clearly an exemplar, eating insects. The reason for this is that monks, even the majority who were quite prepared to grow and cook food, regarded the eating of meat with horror. Vegetarianism was one of the basic premises of the monastic life. When we look closely at later Palestinian monastic practice, we find that a rather different tradition about John the Baptist's diet was known. In the 1220s, the Frankish bishop of Acre, James of Vitry, visited an Orthodox monastery near the Jordan, founded originally in commemoration of the Baptist's ministry. James asked the monks what the unusual vegetable was that they were eating in the refectory, and was told that it was a plant that grew wild everywhere – the locust-bean. The monks also told James that monks in Palestine had always eaten this, in imitation of John the Baptist. Could the locusts supposedly eaten by John have instead been a wild plant? Two other intriguing pieces of evidence from western sources are also suggestive. Godric of Finchale, a twelfth-century English anchorite, is described as eating wild shoots and grasses in his hermitage in County Durham. Many hermits did likewise, so this is not in itself surprising. But Godric's biographer says explicitly that he did this in imitation of John the Baptist. Moreover, we know that before he became a hermit, Godric had been on a pilgrimage to the Holy Land, and observed the practices of native monks and hermits near Jerusalem. It was as a result of these experiences that he himself became an anchorite. So his own monastic diet may have been as near an imitation of the Palestinian hermits as Godric could manage.[15]

How could this misunderstanding have arisen? The Greek word usually translated in English Bibles as 'locusts' is *akrides*, which can mean either the insect or, more commonly, the locust-bean plant. There appear, then, to have been two traditions active about the nature of John's diet. As for the wild honey, again, local

Palestinian tradition suggests that what has been rendered into English as honey (*Mela agria*) was in fact the melagria so beloved of the grazers.

THE PRINCIPLES OF ABSTINENCE AND SELF-MORTIFICATION

The history of monasticism is characterized by the fierce and passionate abandonment of the ordinary comforts of life, and by the insistence that only in such abandonment can virtue lie. Among such comforts, the most obvious and striking are food and drink. Clearly ascetics who followed this ideal understood that eating and drinking was necessary, but they thought that virtue lay in treating it purely as a necessity, rather than as something capable of giving pleasure. The purpose of food and drink was simply to sustain life so that spiritual perfection could be sought without consideration of the body's desires. The principle is explained in a metaphor by one of the most colourful of the desert fathers, John 'the Dwarf':

> A king who wants to take possession of an enemy's city begins by cutting off the water and the food; so his enemies, dying of hunger, submit to him. It is the same with the passions of the flesh: if a man goes about fasting and hungry, the enemies of his soul grow weak.[16]

The virtue of fasting lay not so much in the ability to go without food, which is a physical attribute, as in the victory that such an ability signalled over the senses. Fasting, as a form of self-denial, was not just about how little one could eat or drink, but about how little attention one gave to the need for eating and drinking, or indeed any bodily function. One of the most extreme examples of this attitude is depicted by the seventh-century writer Leontius of Naples in his *Life of Symeon the Holy Fool*. Symeon, after 29 years as an anchorite in the desert near the Dead Sea, goes to the Syrian city of Emesa to live as an 'urban hermit'. The key to his way of life here was playing the fool by indulging in asocial, or sometime anti-social, behaviour so as to expose the shaky morality on which urban society was based. Accepting employment as an assistant to a soup-seller in the market, he first gorged himself, then gave away all the beans used for making the soup to the poor. He ate meat so as to outrage the expectations of the townspeople about how monks should behave; he stripped naked in public and wore his clothes wrapped around his head like a turban; he even squatted down in the market place to defecate when he felt the need. 'It was' says Leontius, 'as though Symeon had no body, and gave no mind to what human convention or nature might consider to be disgraceful behaviour.'[17]

In order to understand how this understanding of the moral value of fasting emerged, it is useful to first examine the roots of the ethical tradition of early Christian asceticism. Throughout monastic literature, especially that of the desert fathers, there runs a deeply ethical thread in which the intention of an action is considered more important than the action itself. This was far from unique to Christian teaching, and the fact that it was adopted so naturally as part of monastic behaviour only demonstrates the debt owed by the early Christian Church to classical and Jewish precursors. The most obvious example of continuity between pre-Christian and early Christian asceticism is the Essene sect in first-century Judaism. Josephus, the Romanized Jewish historian (c.37–100 AD), left the most complete account of the Essenes and their practices known to us.

He described them as a dissident group of Jews who observed the teachings of Moses in particularly rigorous ways. They lived in communes in the Judaean desert near the River Jordan, the location of the most famous of which, Qumran, is famous for the discovery of the so-called Dead Sea Scrolls. They devoted their lives to prayer, worship and simplicity of living, eschewed marriage and sexual relations, and maintained a strict bodily austerity that included dietary restrictions beyond the Mosaic law. Whether Christian monks consciously modelled themselves on the Essenes is highly debatable. Josephus' works became very well known in the Middle

Ages, and in the fourteenth century, when religious orders began
to develop complex theories about the origins of monasticism, the
Essenes were indeed seen as precursors by one such order, the
Carmelite friars. But it is unlikely that, despite obvious similarities
of conduct, many early Christian monks knew enough about the
Essenes to have used them as a model, even had they been inclined
to do so.[18]

Nevertheless, the early Christian monk did conform in some
ways to a familiar type already existing in the late Roman Empire.
Deep religious sentiment was a common feature of the many
religious practices within the Empire. The syncretism of religious
observances in the Empire meant that many ordinary Romans
probably looked on holy men and women who followed quite
different religions in a similar way. For them, what mattered was
not a different set of beliefs, but the same practices. Austerity in
personal behaviour, in the form of chastity, sobriety and moderation in food and all aspects of outward behaviour were standard
ways in which religious people could be identified – whether they
were Neoplatonic philosophers, adherents of the cult of Mithras,
Christians, Jews or Persian fire-worshippers.

A contemporary description of the third-century Neoplatonic
philosopher Plotinus dwelt on his abstemiousness in food and
drink, his custom of wearing old and poor clothing, his long
and unkempt beard, his habit of keeping silence for long periods,
and his capacity for inner withdrawal. It might be a description
of Anthony or any of the founding fathers of Egyptian, Syrian or
Palestinian monasticism. Basil of Caesarea, who brought monasticism to Asia Minor, was a classically educated Roman who saw
no incompatibility between the ethical teachings of Plato and the
Academy and his own Christian upbringing. Athanasius sought
to place Anthony within the educated philosophical tradition
by making his hero debate with a group of philosophers who
sought out the solitary monk to test his wisdom. Anthony's faith
in God, inner strength and mental discipline made him not only
the equal, but the superior of the philosophers, in Athanasius'

view. Subsequently, describing monks as 'philosophers' and their ascetic practices as 'philosophy' became part of the standard repertoire of writers about early monasticism. Some historians have seen in this tendency evidence of the devaluing of 'the life of the mind' altogether in the fourth and fifth centuries, but the point is that asceticism and bodily austerity were seen as entirely appropriate conduct for Christian monks and philosophically inclined adherents of traditional paganism. One branch of classical philosophy, Stoicism, saw asceticism in terms that suggest parallels with the thoughts of John Cassian on the subject. For both Stoics and Cassian, asceticism was a form of training, the purpose of which was for the mind to govern the body.

It is tempting to see this mind–body relationship as one in which the body and its needs are suppressed or relegated to secondary importance. It is true that Christianity followed its parent, Judaism – or, at least, mainstream Judaism – in regarding the soul as eternal in contrast to the mortal body. But, despite the extremes of ascetic behaviour that we encounter in early monasticism, the purpose of fasting or eating very little was not to harm the body, but – surprisingly, perhaps – to perfect it. Here we should remember that the ideal state of humankind was considered to have been that in which it had existed before the Fall and expulsion from the Garden of Eden. In the Garden, the earthly paradise, Adam and Eve had not had to give thought to their bodily needs, because they were provided all around them. The state of dependence on Nature carried with it an abundance that meant no work had to be done in order to feed and clothe oneself. Now, there could be no return to this paradisiacal state of affairs, because the Fall was regarded as an historic event from which there could be no going back. The efforts of the grazers to recapture something of this state of innocence represented an attempt by a few individuals to find some means of personally remaining as free from sin as possible. Not everyone, obviously, could follow this path. Another way of trying to recapture innocence was to live in such a way as to make the body as 'angelic' as possible. Taken literally, this entailed the perfection of the body by the least reliance possible on earthly things, including food. For this reason, the simplest foods were the best, and the body should not take in more than was strictly necessary to support life. Eating too richly, or too much, or devoting a disproportionate amount of time and effort to what one ate, was potentially to pollute the body.

Trying to achieve this angelic state of bodily existence was a matter of balance. To go too far in the direction of abstinence, to the extent that one disregarded the body and its needs altogether, was to despise God's creation. It is significant that the region where bodily asceticism took on its most extreme forms – Syria – was also that closest to and most influenced by the Persian Manichean religion, which proposed a sharp bipolar split between mind and body. Mainstream Christian teaching rejected such a split: one had to take one's body with one, not escape it or reject it altogether.

For this reason, although the ability to fast was a virtue, it could never be an end in itself. An Egyptian desert father, Abba Poemen, known as 'the Shepherd', advised monks to fast, not by refraining from food altogether for certain periods, but instead to eat only very little food daily. Complete fasting, he thought, was ostentatious, because it looked as though one were simply setting achievement tests for oneself. The ideal was to find the critical balance so that one took in just enough to keep the body functioning, but not enough to satisfy a craving for food – if that happened, one was giving in to bodily appetites, rather than controlling them. John Cassian illustrates this in his account of a visit to Abba Serenus in Nitria, when he describes how the monk gave him and his companion to eat, in addition to bread, three olives, a few plums and figs, and a basket of dried peas. 'We took only five,' says John, 'because it seemed wicked to take more.' John Cassian was quite clear that excessive fasting was just as dangerous, spiritually speaking, as excessive eating. 'We should refresh ourselves at the proper time with food and sleep, even if we don't feel like it.'[19]

In another story about the monks of Skete, two solitaries meet one day and cook some lentils to share together, but while they are cooking they begin to sing psalms together, and by the time they had sung their way through the entire Psalter, they had forgotten all about their desire for food. Here, the need for food is overcome by the spiritual satisfaction of shared worship.[20]

The fast should not outweigh other considerations in one's relationship to God or to fellow monks. Poemen would surely have been critical of the monk who declined to break his vow of fasting to eat a dish of prunes and meal that had been prepared for him by another monk to alleviate stomach pains. The refusal to accept hospitality was a mark of obstinacy worse than breaking the vow itself. The example of Paphnutios, quoted earlier, who agreed to drink wine on pain of death when captured by brigands, is another example of the same principle. In his case, he preferred to break his vow rather than see his fellow men commit murder to satisfy his own obstinacy. Excessive fasting, like excess in other feats of austerity, was a sign of pride, and the purpose of the monastic life was to cultivate humility.

Abba Poemen referred to the constant discipline of eating a very small amount every day as 'the royal way'. On one occasion, a visiting monk reproached Poemen for being so weak as to require food every day; after all, Anthony, the first of the monks, had not needed to eat daily. Poemen explained that the purpose of eating was to furnish the minimum amount of nourishment needed to maintain the body in a 'perfect' state – in other words, as an engine of prayer and contemplation. Monks who made a show of going without food just because they could were to be treated with suspicion, because they were allowing their indifference to food to become, in itself, a passion and a source of pride.

KINDS OF FOOD

The Syriac version of Palladius' *Lausiac History* contains a salutary little tale about a monastic 'grazer'. A monk who had lived in and on the edge of the desert for some years, eating only the wild herbs he could gather, one day met a shepherd. The shepherd took from his bag exactly the same kind of wild-growing plants that the monk had been eating, and proceeded to make a meal with them. He told the surprised monk that he had been eating them whenever he was in the wilderness with his flock for thirty years. The monk realized that what he had been practising self-consciously as a virtue was in fact a necessity for those who lived in and on the fringes of the desert, not out of choice, but because this was the life into which they had been born.[21]

Some monks – Symeon the Stylite being an example – came from exactly this socio-economic and geographical background. This is probably true of most of the Coptic-speaking monks of Egypt and many of the Aramaic-speaking Syrian monks. The Greek-speaking monks in Egypt, however, and probably many of the 'foreign' monks who settled in Palestine, were less likely to come from this background: Basil, for example, was from a prominent land-owning family in Cappadocia; Arsenius had been a minister at the imperial court in Constantinople before retiring to Skete; and Anthony, Sabas, Euthymius and others seem to have been born to prosperous families. Monks such as these made conscious choices to live in poverty and self-denial. Grazing off wild-growing food represented a sacrifice of austerity for them.

Peasant families in Egypt, Syria and Palestine were used to sup-plementing food that they grew or bought with 'free' wild-growing food. For such families, the normal daily diet was based on beans, lentils and other pulses, supplemented by olives and olive oil, vegetables and herbs, dates and cheese. As we shall see, the same is true, with obvious regional variations – butter and fat replacing oil, for example, in the north – in medieval Europe. One has to consider, therefore, whether the monastic life really constituted a drastic change in diet for many of these hermits and monks. The social reality was that diet, for all save the very wealthy, was limited by availability and by the cost of long-distance imports. Most people at most times ate what could be grown and produced within a locality defined by a day's walk. The typical foods that formed the staple of desert monks – flat bread, cheese, olives, leeks or onions – were the same as those described by the 19th-century explorer of Arabia Charles Doughty, as forming the staple of Arab families making the pilgrimage from Damascus to Mecca.

The staple diet of monks in the eastern Mediterranean can be seen in an episode from Cyril of Scythopolis' *Life of Sabas*. At a time of general famine, the monks in the Great Laura were saved by emergency supplies sent from Jerusalem. These comprised the flat small loaves characteristic of the region, grain in its raw state, olive oil, cheese and wine. In another episode, a monk of the Great Laura who had spent Lent in solitude found himself at Easter with nothing but roots to eat, until he received a surprise visit from a stranger with a gift of white bread, olive oil, cheese, eggs, honey and wine. (The white bread, of course, was a great luxury, made

Slow-cooked lentils

The essential equipment for this recipe is an earthenware pot or jar with handles on either side. Half fill with dried lentils that have previously been soaked in cold water overnight and drained, then add cold water to the top of the jar and put it on an open fire or in the oven. Allow the jar to come to the boil and cook gently for about 20 minutes, until the water has been absorbed by the lentils. Meanwhile, bring another pot of water slowly to the boil, and add fresh water, at simmering point, to the jar of lentils. Repeat this process as the water boils away until the lentils are soft. Add salt and strain, keeping some of the cooking liquor. Heat a generous amount of olive oil in a deep wide-bottomed saucepan, and, on low to medium heat, add diced peppers, a sliced onion, two crushed garlic cloves and a little chilli. When the onion becomes translucent, add the lentils and stir them around in the oil, then the cooking liquor. After another minute, remove from heat and serve.

Split peas, dried beans or chickpeas can be used instead of lentils.

with flour rather than barley or ground lentils.) That these foods had to be sent obviously indicates that the monks had exhausted their own supplies. But what kind of foods could they have produced and eaten in a time free of famine? Pachomius' monasteries along the Nile in Upper Egypt were, in one sense, giant collective farms. The monks took turns at various kinds of manual labour that included growing vegetables: mostly beans and other legumes, but also radishes, onions, leeks and garlic. Mention is made in the *Rule of Pachomius* of drovers and shepherds in the employ of the monasteries. The animals under their care were kept for milk for making cheese, as well as for hides and wool. Of course, according to the *Rule*, meat was not to be eaten at all. Fish was eaten, in particular the small salt fish of the Nile, but also fish imported from the Red Sea. Throughout the Roman Empire a kind of fish paste, garum, was widespread, and its popularity continued in Byzantine kitchens. Fresh fruit were cultivated in monastery orchards – in Egypt, mostly dates but also plantains and the ubiquitous figs, and elsewhere in the Mediterranean, apples, grapes and plums.[22]

A book on monks' and hermits' food should not really need to discuss meat at all, since animal flesh was forbidden in most monastic rules and customaries, except for the sick, and eschewed by most solitaries. The *Rule of Benedict* forbad eating the flesh of four-footed animals, and in doing so it summed up the ideals and practices of most earlier monastic rules. In fact, this prohibition probably did not seem quite as difficult to bear as it might in our society. Meat was a luxury for most Mediterranean people, and as such, for monks to have eaten it would have given entirely the wrong signal. Besides this, the economic reality of monastic life made it implausible, for it would have entailed the expense of raising livestock and keeping herds in pasture. However, Macarius sanctioned the inclusion of a scrap of meat if it was available in a lentil stew.

Such morsels were probably provided as gifts rather than coming from animals kept by the monks themselves. Hilarion, when living in Cyprus, was once invited to share a meal by Epiphanius, bishop of Salamis, and was appalled to be offered a dish of chicken. He refused it, saying that in fifty years of monastic life he had never once eaten meat, and that it was not his custom to do so. The bishop replied that it was not his custom to argue with his guests or to force his hospitality on them. Shamed by this gracious reply, Hilarion observed, 'that is a better custom than mine', and accepted the chicken. This story is echoed in the belief of the eleventh-century reformer John Gualbert that meat could be eaten if it were given to hermits, and if nothing else were available. On the other hand, an anecdote in the *Sayings of the Fathers* reports approvingly of an episode involving Theophilus, the fourth-century arch-bishop of Alexandria. Theophilus had invited a group of monks to Alexandria for a bout of pagan temple-destruction – a pursuit that the monks of Upper Egypt seem to have particularly enjoyed. As the monks sat down to dinner with the archbishop, a dish of stew was brought in which they began to eat. The archbishop respectfully helped the elderly monk next to him to a choice piece of veal, saying, 'Here, have this nice piece of meat, Father.' The monk, horrified, exclaimed that they thought they were eating a vegetable dish, and that they would never have knowingly eaten meat; they refused to touch another mouthful.

In the instructional literature written by reforming monks of the twelfth century, meat-eating was seen as a particularly powerful example of the difference between monasticism and the worldly life outside the cloister. An anecdote in the *Book of Miracles* com-piled by Herbert of Clairvaux in the late twelfth century bears this out. A novice monk at Clairvaux, Achard, has been entrusted with a prophecy that one of his fellow novices will give up the monastic life altogether. Desperate to prevent this, Achard stays up all night in prayer in the dormitory, but can only watch helplessly as two huge demons carry in a roast chicken and hold it over the heads of the sleeping novices to tempt them with the rich aroma of cooked meat. To make the point clear, a snake has entwined itself around the chicken. Sure enough, one of the novices later decides he can no longer bear the sacrifices demanded by monastic life and leaves

Clairvaux; not without a certain grim satisfaction, Herbert adds that the lapsed novice later went mad.[23]

Bread and Dates

The most fundamental food was bread. As we have seen, Anthony took a supply of bread and salt with him into the desert – salt, presumably, to replenish what his body would lose in perspiration in the desert, and bread for the basic supply of protein needed to survive. Every cenobitic monastery and laura in Palestine seems to have had its own bakery – basically, a bread oven – and at Skete a number of such ovens provided for groups of cells. The importance of bread to desert monasteries is clear from the fact that bread ovens or bakeries were built wherever a group of monks settled. Cyril of Scythopolis' *Life of Sabas* tells us that a bakery was the first building to be erected after the church in any new laura or monastery. Typically, these bakeries were wood-fuelled ovens in which, after the heat required to bake the bread had cooled, other foods might be cooked. In Skete, bread ovens were communal enterprises, and monks could take their dough to be baked into loaves several at a time, so that they would not have to leave their cell for days on end. At the other great Egyptian monastic enterprise of Nitria, where monks lived either alone, in pairs or in small groups, there were in Palladius' time about 5,000 monks, whose needs were all served by just seven bakeries. Presumably this was possible because baking was done in bulk and in advance, so that each monk would need to send dough to the bakery infrequently. One episode in the *Life of Sabas* shows us the baker in a monastery in Asia Minor using the oven to dry his clothes as it cooled at the end of a rainy day. (When he forgot his clothes and lit the oven next morning, it was Sabas who jumped into the oven to rescue them before they were burnt to cinders.)[24]

In Pachomius' monasteries, the bakery was a place of ritualized work. Unlike the smaller bakeries of Palestinian lauras, Pachomius' large monasteries had huge bakeries in which teams of monks worked in rotation to bake the amounts of bread required by

2.   Bread oven. Tintern Abbey kitchens, Monmouthshire

hundreds of monks. A kind of production line was established, with some monks mixing the flour and water, others kneading in a kneading-trough, and others putting the loaves in the oven. Making bread was, of course, vital for the maintenance of the community, since it was the staple food. For this reason, it also became a symbol of the community's sense of purpose. The *Regulations of Horsiesios*, a document that preserves much of Pachomius' original precepts, begins the section on bread-making with the exhortation: 'When the time has come to make our small quantity of bread, all of us, great and little, must work at making bread in the fear of God and with great understanding, reciting the word of God with gravity, without pride, boasting or respect of persons.' All the bread had to be of the same grade and type; no monk might bake a different kind of bread for himself. Monks were assigned according to aptitude for the tasks of grinding and milling the grain, for kneading, and for baking. Separate regulations were issued for the team of monks who were required to knead. Each monk was given a kneading trough and a basket of flour; at a signal from the head baker, the monks began to knead, but carefully so as to avoid spilling water on the feet of other monks; as they kneaded, they were to recite psalms softly. They were to take care not to leave any dough behind in the trough, and each monk had to wash his trough after the work was finished.[25]

The work was carried out in strict silence. In one version of the *Life of Pachomius,* the founder gave his deputy Theodore three weeks' penance for letting the monks in the bakery chatter while at their work. Pachomius had left Theodore in charge at Tabennesi while he supervised the establishment of the new monastery

3.   Bread kneading trough. St John the Theologian, Patmos

at Phbow. At this stage, Phbow did not yet have a bakery, so Pachomius went back to Tabennesi to supervise the baking of the loaves for Phbow for the coming year. An angel reported to him that a monk had broken his rule by asking out loud for water for the kneading of the dough, instead of simply beating his hand on the side of the kneading trough in the agreed signal, as Pachomius' *Rule* instructed. Pachomius held Theodore responsible, and when his investigation into the matter revealed that in all no fewer than eighteen monks had talked in the bakery, he forced Theodore to turn over charge of the bakery to him directly. Besides talking in the bakery, Pachomius also prohibited any monk from going there without being ordered to do so. No monk was to loiter in the oven-house when bakers were at work. This strictness may have had cultural origins. For some reason, bakers seem to have had a shady reputation in Egypt. They were regarded as being garrulous, hard-living and generally unreliable. The *Life of Pachomius* tells the story of a new recruit, who had himself been a baker before entering Tabennesi, giving the following warning to Theodore: 'If you go to the bakery to make bread, and you see one of the brothers joking or playing around, do not be surprised. It is inevitable that you will find all sorts of people in a group of bakers.' This seems to have been one area in which Palestinian practice differed from Egyptian. In the Palestinian tradition, where monks rotated their tasks on a monthly basis, work in the bakery was less specialized and seen as one of the more menial forms of labour.[26]

Typically, the bread eaten by Eastern monks was a flat unleavened kind similar to the 'pita' of the eastern Mediterranean region today. Its ingredients were simply wheat flour and water. The 'loaf' sometimes referred to in the sources was probably quite small. Cassian tells us that the monks of Skete ate two and a half of these daily. A Syriac source indicates that monks who were fasting might eat two daily, whereas the normal ration was ten – which suggests that they were in fact the size of small bread rolls. The *Rule of Pachomius* specifies that fasting monks who ate by themselves rather than communally should have especially small loaves made for them. Frequent reference to salt eaten with the bread suggests that salt was not normally included in the dough before baking. The implication of the story of Theodore in the *Life of Pachomius* is that this kind of bread, being unleavened and therefore without any agent to make it rise, lasted long enough to make the whole baking process an annual event. A huge quantity of loaves must have been baked in a given period once a year. In the dry heat of Upper Egypt, this bread would have dried out quickly, but could be stored in such a way that it did not rot or go mouldy. When it was needed, it was softened with water to make it palatable again.

The anonymous *Life of Macarius*, who was one of the pioneers of the Egyptian desert, mentions a food known as 'triticum spelta'. This seems to have been a kind of wheat flour mash, adopted by monks living in very hot climates who had limited or no access to a bread oven. Flour or any other kind of grain was mixed with water to produce a dough that could be added to a stew or ragout of lentils or beans, or, in extreme need, eaten simply with salt. In the *Life of Anthony*, Anthony makes his bread without an oven simply by leaving the flour-and-water paste out to dry in the sun. This recalls a traditional kind of Finnish bread, made by drying strips of dough under the ceiling – presumably a custom originating from houses in which a fire in the centre of the room would send smoke upwards through a hole in the roof. The French traveller Jules Leroy found Coptic monks at the desert monastery of St Anthony, near the Red Sea, doing essentially the same to make their bread in the 1950s.

The Beduin observed by Doughty in Arabia made flat bread by cooking the flour-and-water paste in strips over an open fire. The Victorian traveller also encountered a standard peasant dish made from grain dried and toasted in the sun, then boiled in water to yield a mash. Sometimes the early monks used other grains, when no wheat flour was available: lentil bread and barley bread are both mentioned in the Syriac collection *The Paradise of the Fathers*. Bread was made with a variety of grains – wheat, barley, oats or corn, depending on what grew most naturally in the region. Indeed, any wild grain or grass, including crab grass, could be used, since no wild grain is known to be poisonous. The grass sometimes known as foxtail, because of its distinctive long hairs, which is widespread throughout Asia and Africa, can be eaten raw or boiled, and can also be ground into a grain for making bread.

Something of the ritual quality of bread in the monastic diet is indicated in the *Life of Pachomius*, not only in the rules of behaviour in the bakery, but also in a bread-related miracle. Pachomius gave a small loaf to a boy who had been possessed by a demon; he hoped the bread would cure the boy, but the boy refused to eat it. The boy's father broke the bread into small pieces which he stuffed into balls of cheese and dates, but the boy, seeing through this ruse, removed the bread and ate the rest of the food. Finally the father starved the boy for two days, then served him a porridge into which the bread had been mixed; on eating it, the boy was cured.

It is time to consider Onuphrios and his dates. According to tradition, the Egyptian hermit Onuphrios was discovered living in solitude in the desert, and surviving solely on the dates that grew on the palm tree under whose shade he was accustomed to rest. As he explained, the tree provided all his wants: each month a fresh bunch, sufficient for a daily supply, fell into his lap. Dates certainly played an important role in the diet of the Mediterranean monks and hermits. They feature on the menus of most Byzantine monastic rules from the Middle Ages, and had the advantage of being permitted food during Lent. Dates receive more attention than any other produce in the *Rule of Pachomius*, which was highly influential to later generations. The date was supposedly the only food used by an anonymous monk of Skete as a means of battling demons. Settling on fasting as the best way to rid himself of the demon, the monk sustained himself by chewing date stones, so as to extract the nutritional juices from the fruit while keeping his strict fast.[27]

Could one survive on such a limited diet – regardless of whether such monotony would drive the monk to distraction? If a monk set out to live off one kind of food alone, he could hardly pick a more versatile one. The date palm, *Phoenix dactylifera*, has been estimated to have eight hundred distinct uses. Some of them are culinary; others, like the use of the leaves to weave baskets, are attested in the literature of the Egyptian desert fathers. Date palms generally comprise leaves in five distinct sections, which grow higher each year as new growth comes in. The older leaves eventually die, but since they have a life of about five years, this is a slow process, and fully-grown trees can reach up to thirty metres in height – entirely large enough to provide Onuphrios with plenty of shade. Onuphrios apparently told his enquirers that the tree's monthly bunches provided all the fruit he needed. Typically, an average annual yield from a commercial tree is about a hundred pounds of fruit, though it can be as much as twice or more. The bunches weigh over twenty pounds, and can contain a thousand dates each.

The fruit itself provides both food and drink, and Onuphrios may, with some imagination and know-how, have varied his diet beyond simply eating the fruit whole. The ninth-century monastic *Rule of Theodore the Studite* mentions a date wine made from the fermented juice of the fruit. It would have taken some effort to produce this, but Onuphrios might have been able to fashion a machine of some basic type to help him. The bole or kernel of the tree can also be crushed to produce a sap or syrup, or even ground into a flour-like sago. The fruit can be dried and ground into a kind of flour, which when mixed with water and other grains such as barley produces a cake. The native palm of the Indonesian archipelago yields a yellow flour that forms the staple diet of the Moluccas and other Pacific islands. The leaves can also be used, as for example by the Egyptian monk John Kolobos, for thatching a hut, or covering the entrance to a cell.

Dates are rich in sugar and fats and contain vitamins A, B and B_2. If they cannot quite sustain life by themselves, they do provide most of the necessary nutrients. Beduin have survived for centuries for long periods in the desert on dates and camel milk. There are now as many as six hundred varieties of date, but in the early Christian period this would have been a far lower number.

However, Onuphrios' date palm would have needed to be female, for only these produce fruit. Besides the date palm itself, there are other varieties of palm that produce edible fruit, such as *Ziziphus spina-christi*, known to Beduin as *sidr*, and *Ziziphus leucodermis* or haybed, both of which are related to the jujube. Another palm, *Nannorrhops ritchieana*, which is better known for its strong fibres, yields a fruit, known locally as *mish*, that can be ground up into a mash and stored for several months. Onuphrios' diet, if he was wholly reliant on palm trees, will not have been varied, but it probably represents an extreme version of what, over many centuries, many inhabitants of the Arabian desert lived off for long periods.

Chapter Three

The 'hermit craze' of the Middle Ages

WESTERN MONASTICISM AND THE REDISCOVERY OF 'THE DESERT'

Monastic ideals had been imported to the West from Egypt through the writings of John Cassian and the translations of Basil's writings into Latin at the end of the fourth and the beginning of the fifth century. As we have seen, Benedict's *Rule* (c.565) relied on these existing traditions, and Benedict certainly knew Egyptian monasticism from Cassian's two works, the *Institutes* and *Conferences*. By c.600, Benedict's model for cenobitic monasteries had reached Rome, perhaps from monks fleeing from political upheaval. The pope, Gregory I, was so impressed by what he learnt of Benedict's monastic experiment at Monte Cassino that he set out to find out as much as he could about the founder and wrote an account of his life and miracles in his own rather rambling *Dialogues*.

Although cenobitic monasticism became the norm in Western Europe in the early Middle Ages, Benedict's *Rule* did not enjoy unchallenged dominance, and there were always monastic houses, not to mention individual monks, who chose other ways. One such was the tradition of Irish monasticism that emerged in the sixth century. Christianity had arrived in Ireland in the fifth century largely through the missionary work of Patrick, a Roman from Britain. From the sixth century onward, a rigorous form of cenobitic life was implanted in south-western Scotland by the Irishman Columba; it began to spread in continental Europe from the seventh century under the influence of Columbanus. Irish monasticism was typically more disciplinarian than Benedictine, with considerable emphasis on penitential observances by the monks. Irish monks developed a reputation for learning, but also for wandering from one monastery to another, something of which Benedict had strongly disapproved. Just as in its original heartland of the eastern Mediterranean, a strong tradition of solitary monasticism also developed in Ireland, and spread from there into northern England. Here, the two traditions, Celtic and Benedictine, developed together after the conversion of the pagan Anglo-Saxons began in the sixth century. Although Roman influence eventually dominated, some features of Celtic monasticism never entirely died out. Scottish and northern English solitaries in the Middle Ages continued to demonstrate some of these, such as a close interest in Nature and animal life.

Even where Benedict's *Rule* was officially followed, monasteries developed in ways that would have surprised Benedict himself. This is partly because his template was flexible enough to allow a number of variations according to local custom. It was also, however, because monasteries began to perform functions for society as a whole. Some of these were practical; for example, monasteries, as self-sufficient communities, often had surpluses of food that they could distribute to the poor. Moreover, in a predominantly rural society, monasteries unwittingly fostered population growth around them as they attracted what today we would call 'service industries'. Many monasteries, having initially been founded in unsettled areas, became urban centres as towns grew around them. Monasteries were also providers of education, since the correct observance of the liturgy demanded literacy. In theory, every bishopric had to have a cathedral school providing advanced education, but in rural areas monasteries were often the only recourse for teaching anything more advanced than basic literacy. Moreover, since more educated people could be found in monasteries than anywhere else, it was often here that rulers turned for advice and for such civil services as they needed to run their administrations. But the most important way in which monasteries served society was in the reciprocal relationship they offered for security in the afterlife.

One of the clearest examples of how this relationship was supposed to work comes from the deed drawn up by the founder of the monastery that was to become the most famous and powerful in the whole of western Europe: Cluny. In 910, the duke of the rambling duchy of Aquitaine, William, gave land and property in southern Burgundy to a small group of monks, led by one Berno. The deed or 'charter' transferring the land and property to the monks became a model for such transactions for future generations and centuries. William acknowledged his sinful state, accepting that such a state was indeed the likely outcome for anyone engaged in political life. He regretted his inability to live the life of true penitence and prayer that would ensure his salvation. However, he expressed the hope that by making it possible for a group of monks to live such a life – in other words, by founding the monastery of Cluny and endowing the monks with sufficient material support to enable them to be independent of any other earthly power – he might be able to share in the salvation that the monks would surely earn through their pursuit of the monastic life.[1] This was, in effect, a transaction: William donated land and property sufficient to provide an income for the monastery; in return, the monks installed William and his family in their liturgical celebrations, so that they would have prayers said on their behalf as long as the monastery lasted. Spiritual help was the return for William's investment in worldly goods. The principle of the reciprocal relationship was that the monks who were enabled to ensure that they gained salvation by the sacrifice of their own lives to God did so on behalf of founders and patrons such as William. It was very far from what Benedict – let alone the desert fathers of Egypt, Syria and Palestine – had envisaged, but it was an arrangement that suited early medieval society.

When it was founded, Cluny was unusual for its day in that it managed to retain complete independence from any other authority save the papacy. This is probably how Benedict had seen cenobitic monasticism working, with each monastic community providing for its own needs from a combination of its own manual labour and some gifts from benefactors. But by the tenth century, many monasteries in both the eastern Mediterranean and Western Europe were, in practice, dependent on the aristocracy. Kings, queens and nobles who founded monasteries naturally tended to retain an interest in their foundations. In many cases this amounted to a proprietorial attitude towards the monastery as an institution – and, most important, towards its property. Thus, it is not at all uncommon to find both early medieval Western and Byzantine monasteries and convents having abbots or abbesses imposed on them by the founding family; sometimes the abbot was not even a monk himself but simply a member of the founding family. In such circumstances, it was easy for founding families to siphon off or treat as their own the income generated by the monastery from its landed properties. At its least intrusive, this might take the form of extended visits on the part of the founding family and its household, on which they would of course be fed and maintained at the monastery's expense. At its most extreme, as for example in the Byzantine system known as the *charistike*, in which a layman was appointed as 'protector' of the monastery's property, it might amount to straightforward embezzlement.

The founding of Cluny represents an attempt to reform this situation by retaining control over all property and the rights that accompanied property-ownership in the hands of the monastery. Duke William of Aquitaine willingly surrendered any rights in the monastery. By the 1060s, Cluny was by far the most influential and the largest monastery in the West. A new building programme was launched by Abbot Hugh the Great (1024–1109). The result was an abbey church able to accommodate three hundred monks; it was larger than any church in the West save St Peter's in Rome.

By this date, however, a new wave of reform had begun in both Byzantine and Western monasticism. Although they had rather different origins and took different forms, at root many of their concerns were the same. Principally, reformers worried that secular powers had too much control over monasteries, and that the monasteries themselves, as large corporate property-owners, had lost sight of the basic principles of founders like Basil and Benedict – let alone of the desert fathers. Consequently, in the eleventh century interest in early forms of monastic living was revived, and this resulted in new attempts to imitate the style of life of the desert fathers. Some reformers, such as Peter Damian and Romuald in Italy, were probably influenced by contemporary practices among Orthodox monks in the Greek-speaking parts of southern Italy. In the poor rural provinces of Calabria and Apulia, still nominally part of the Byzantine Empire, but in fact in the process of being brought under the control of the new Norman settlers, monasticism was still highly fluid. Monks like St Nilus of Rossano offered examples of solitary monasticism that were in many ways throwbacks to the golden age of the early monks of the eastern Mediterranean. Moreover, Nilus was admired by western Catholics as well as by Orthodox churchmen.

The critical factor in the revival of early monastic ideals in the eleventh and twelfth centuries was, however, education. A cultural movement sometimes known by historians as 'the twelfth-century Renaissance' began in the monasteries, with the revival of classical reading and writing. On the whole, what monks read was not so much the classics of ancient literature – though that was also a feature of this Renaissance – as the Christian classics in Latin: the writings of Augustine, Ambrose, Jerome, Gregory the Great, Boethius, Cassiodorus and John Cassian. From these, and especially Jerome and Cassian, monks learnt what had been forgotten over the centuries: how the first monks had lived. New manuscripts of Cassian's *Conferences* and *Institutes*, of the *Sayings of the Fathers* and the *Life of Anthony* and related works from this period provide evidence of this new interest – as monks read old works, they made copies of them so that they could be disseminated more widely. (In the Byzantine world, this had never really been lost, but even so there is increased evidence for interest in Basil, Palladius and other works relating to early monasticism.)

Reading John Cassian's descriptions of the Egyptian fathers promoted the ideal of a return to the original simplicity of monastic life, characterized by the pursuit of solitude, detachment from settled society and asceticism. Although Benedict's *Rule* advised against solitary monasticism for the inexperienced, many reforming monks of the late eleventh and early twelfth centuries began as solitaries before attracting followers and founding communities of their own. They were reacting against what they saw as slipping standards in the Church and monasteries of their day, in which the *Rule of Benedict* was often ignored or bypassed by local customs that permitted monks greater comforts than he had recommended. The sense of decline is well expressed by Guibert of Nogent, whom we met in Chapter One. An oblate himself, Guibert worried that the large number of monks who had grown up in monasteries from childhood without knowing any other life was in fact detrimental to monasticism as a whole. Such monks imagined that because they had enjoyed less chance to lead sinful lives than people in secular life, they needed to do very little to ensure their salvation. Many monasteries, he observed, were sunk in complacency and idleness as a result.[2] This was what many reformers at the time wanted to change, and they did so by leaving established monasteries and founding new ones in poverty and seclusion in remote places that they themselves called 'deserts', in obvious reference to the desert fathers of Egypt and Palestine.

In 1098, a small such reforming community was founded amid turmoil and resentment in northern Burgundy. A small group of monks left the established monastery of Molesme – itself only a generation old – along with their abbot, Robert, after a bitter argument between two factions among the monks, those who wanted to embrace reform and the majority, who were opposed to it. They settled in a wilderness on land not under cultivation and therefore unsettled. Initially called simply 'the New Monastery' by the dissidents, the new community was to become known as Cîteaux, and it was here that the reform movement found its spearhead.

The circumstances of the founding of Cîteaux were described in the 1130s by a Benedictine monk from Normandy, Orderic Vitalis. Sceptical of the reformers' intentions, Orderic presented a colourful version of the quarrel between Abbot Robert and the anti-reform majority at Molesme. Robert urged his monks to return to the fundamentals of the *Rule of Benedict*, and to observe its prescriptions literally. We should live, he told them, as far as possible like Anthony, Macarius and the other desert fathers. The opposing party scornfully replied that they lived in France, not the Egyptian desert, and that it was foolish to adopt an artificial lifestyle to which neither the climate, nor landscape, were suited.[3] Moreover, they insisted, the point of Benedict's *Rule* was that it was flexible enough to allow for modifications to suit local circumstances. Should they adopt the costume of the desert even in cold northern climates? Or insist on using olive oil even in regions where lard or butter was produced locally just because, as an Italian, Benedict had referred to the use of oil? Most tellingly, they argued that the changes that had occurred in monastic life since Benedict wrote his *Rule* should not be despised or disregarded, but embraced as part of the organic and natural growth of society. Thus, where Benedict had prescribed a pound of bread and a pint of beans as the daily ration for each monk, there was in fact nothing wrong with eating a more varied diet than this, and in larger quantities, if the monastery's resources could afford it.

The most articulate exponent of the reform at Cîteaux was Bernard of Clairvaux (1090–1153). Born a younger son into a family of minor nobility in Burgundy, Bernard entered Cîteaux as a young man in 1112. Naturally endowed with the gift of persuasion, Bernard brought with him some of his relatives, including his eldest brother, Guy, whom he had successfully urged to leave his wife for the sake of Cîteaux. In 1115, Bernard was sent to found Clairvaux, also in Burgundy. The new monastery was dependent on Cîteaux, and represented the characteristic feature of Cistercian monasticism that was to make it so successful: the 'daughter-house'. The Cistercians saw their monasteries as a single association of communities, all of which subscribed to the same reforming ideals: Benedictine simplicity of life, and remoteness from centres of habitation and austerity. By the mid-1120s, Bernard's eloquence was finding new targets among the older established Benedictine monasteries. His particular ire was reserved for the greatest of all: Cluny.

ST BERNARD, CLUNY AND FOOD

The quarrel began when a young cousin of Bernard's, Robert of Châtillon, who had already joined Clairvaux as a novice, left before taking his vows in order to enter Cluny. From a letter that Bernard wrote to him in 1124, we learn that Robert's reason for doing so was that he had been promised in childhood as an oblate to Cluny and that, now that it was time for him to take vows, he was reminded of this commitment made on his behalf by his parents. Bernard was clearly furious, but his letter is a rhetorical masterpiece, blending by turns sorrow at having failed to see how unhappy his young relation must have been at Clairvaux, resentment at the behaviour of Cluny in luring him away with empty promises, and scorn for the way that the *Rule of Benedict* was followed at Cluny. He accused the Cluniacs of living far too grandly, and in particular of too much concern for fine food. 'The soul is not fattened out of frying pans', he observed in a characteristically excoriating shaft.[4]

At the instigation of a reform-minded Benedictine friend, William, abbot of St Thierry, Bernard expanded on his theme in a separate treatise, known as the *Apologia for Abbot William*. Here he developed the critique of Cluniac eating habits. At Cluny – and, by implication, other monasteries that had been influenced by Cluniac practices – 'course after course is brought in' at mealtimes. Because even the Clunaics would not stoop to eating the forbidden meat, they compensated by doubling the fish dishes. These are of such quantity and variety that 'you only have to begin sampling the second dish to imagine that you have never tasted fish before'. Bernard is particularly critical of the chef's art of concealment and disguise. Lest the monks grow tired of the same basic dishes, the food at Cluny is subjected to all kinds of treatment, such as the addition of new and exotic relishes and ingredients, to make it more alluring and, above all, to promote appetite among men who should have no concern for such things. 'Food in its pure state holds no attraction, so we mix together ingredients willy-nilly; we despise the natural goodness that God gave us, and use exotic flavours to stimulate our appetites. In this way we can eat more than we need, and still enjoy it.' He is also critical of the elaboration of the appearance of food, with the intention of pleasing the eye as well as the appetite. 'Unfortunate stomach! The eyes feast on colour, the palate on taste, but the poor stomach, indifferent to either but compelled to accept both, is crushed rather than refreshed in consequence.' Bernard warms to his task when he considers the use to which eggs are put in the monastic kitchen. Eggs, indeed, seem to enrage him like no other food. Who, he asks rhetorically, could list all the ways in which eggs are mistreated by monastic cooks? They are tossed and turned in the pan, subjected to softening or hardening, served in so many unnecessary ways – fried, baked, even stuffed, combined with other foods or on their own.[5]

How much of this alleged Cluniac self-indulgence was in fact true? Probably Cluny was not unusual among large and well-endowed monasteries in feeding its monks with rather more attention to appetite than Benedict's *Rule* had intended. Gerald of Wales, a later twelfth-century writer, tells the story of how the monks of St Swithun's in Winchester, in distress at the bishop's threat to reduce the number of dishes at their dinner by three, petitioned Henry II to intervene. The king asked how many dishes that would leave, and the monks admitted ten. Henry exclaimed that he was never served more than three at one meal, and cursed the bishop if he didn't reduce the monks' dinner to the same number. Gerald was admittedly prone to exaggeration, and never one to pass up the chance of a good story. He may have been right about St Swithun's, though, because at dinner on 13 July 1493 the monks were served an hors d'oeuvre of 'moyle' (warmed bread soaked in the juices of roasting meat from the spit), followed by 'morterells' (meatballs made from white meat), beef and mutton. No fewer than 280 eggs were used in the cooking of this dinner. In another episode, Gerald recounts his own experience of dining at Canterbury. No fewer than sixteen dishes were served, all of them delicacies. Whereas Bernard derided the many ways of serving eggs at Cluny, at Canterbury it was the variety of fish dishes that amazed Gerald. Roast fish, boiled fish, stuffed fish, fried fish; then dishes cooked with so many flavourings and condiments that they awakened rather than sated the appetite. At each table herbs were placed on the table as condiments, but the dishes themselves were so carefully prepared that extra flavouring was not needed.[6]

Some phrases in this passage appear suspiciously close to Bernard's own critique of the Cluniacs, and it may be that Gerald was repeating a well-worn motif in ecclesiastical criticism. His intention is certainly to compare unfavourably the eating habits in monasteries of his day with those of the 'golden age' of monasticism. What would Anthony, or Benedict, the father and founder of monastic life, say to this? he asks rhetorically.

It must be admitted that Bernard does not always appear, either in his writings or in his dealings with other people, in an altogether sympathetic light. But he does seem to have stuck to his principles. He has been criticized for many things, but never for hypocrisy in the matter of his personal asceticism. After his death, a rather curious composite biography, the *First Life of Bernard*, was written about him. William of St Thierry, who had known him longer than most people by the time Bernard died, contributed a vivid and striking portrait of his friend. Bernard's face, according to William, shone with an inner radiance, though he was slight and spare in physique. His hair and beard were naturally reddish, but had begun to turn grey in his last years. 'This treasure,' William remarked, 'was housed in an earthenware vessel.' Among the illnesses to which he became prone was a throat condition that made it difficult for him to swallow. This may have been a muscular problem, possibly arising from mild paralysis of the face. At any rate, it prevented Bernard from eating any dry food, or from taking anything more than small quantities of solid food. In addition, he also suffered from a stomach complaint and from what William calls weakness of the bowel. This may have been something like irritable bowel syndrome; coupled with his throat problem, it combined to make eating difficult and unpleasant for Bernard. His usual food, toward the end of his life, was 'a mouthful of bread, softened with warm water' and a little vegetable broth. Even this, according to William, was too much for his digestion, and he was often unable to keep it down. 'Eating spelled danger for him and digestion pain, but throwing it up caused him misery.' He was not alone among reforming monks in this affliction; a contemporary in the Holy Land, Elias of Narbonne, swallowed only small mouthfuls of bread at table, but used to vomit them up again because his digestion was so weak. Apparently, this was the only thing that kept him from falling asleep at mealtimes, for another of his ascetic practices was to stay awake all night in vigils of prayer.[7]

Was Bernard's digestive trouble the reason for his apparent impatience with monks who overate, and with monastic communities where food was too greatly prized? Was Bernard reacting psychologically against the enjoyment of something that he could never himself enjoy? It is difficult to be sure whether these ailments dogged Bernard throughout his adult life, or developed only later in life. The bowel complaint echoes Jerome's observation of Hilarion's digestive problems in later life as a result of his ascetic eating regime in youth. As such, it may be William of St Thierry's way of signalling to his readers that Bernard was in this respect the equal of Hilarion. If so, then it is another example of the conscious debt owed by the reformers of the twelfth century to the desert fathers. But William's real intention is not to show that Bernard was hostile to food, but rather that he simply did not care about it. His observation that from his youth Bernard avoided any food that had a particularly tempting appearance or flavour seems to recall Bernard's own attack on Cluniac monks for the fault of paying too much heed to taste or smell. According to William, Bernard 'tried to abolish his own capacity to distinguish between tastes'. In other words, Bernard tried consciously to develop an unrefined palate and sense of taste, so as to be indifferent to food.

It is difficult to know whether to read this as a confirmation of Bernard's own exhortations in the letter to Robert and the *Apologia to Abbot William*, or to see it as a more cynical piece of manipulation on William's part – an attempt to portray Bernard as the exemplar of the virtues he had espoused.

One little detail in William's portrait seems to give it verisimilitude. William says that often Bernard drank a liquid by mistake, thinking it was something else. On one occasion, he even drank from a cup of olive oil that had been presented to him by mistake, and apparently did not himself see anything amiss. Only when another monk remarked on the fact that his lips were glistening with the oil did anyone notice the mistake. This reads as though Bernard was so abstracted in his thoughts that he could not even tell what he was ingesting. The olive oil was probably placed on the table as a dressing for a plain vegetable dish, and Bernard mistook it for water. But olive oil, as we now know, is a remarkably healthy food, containing 75 per cent monounsaturated fatty acids and no cholesterol. Moreover, drinking a little olive oil is also a remedy well known in Mediterranean regions for heartburn and digestive complaints. Perhaps Bernard was as oblivious as William makes him out, but he could hardly have chosen a better food for his condition.

MONASTIC MENUS

In a famous account of the early days of Rievaulx, a Cistercian abbey founded in north Yorkshire in 1132, the twelfth-century monk Walter Daniel describes the monks' diet as 'a pound of bread and a pint of beans daily'. In fact, this is exactly what Benedict had prescribed as the staple food in his *Rule*. Benedict, however, was more concerned with quantity and measure than with precise types of food. The basic provision was as follows: monasteries were to provide one main meal every day of the year, and, between Easter and mid-September, a further evening meal. Breakfast was a light meal, usually bread and either wine or beer, depending on the

normal drink of the region. There were some variations depending
on the cycle of liturgical feasts – for example, after Pentecost, the
evening meal was dropped on Wednesdays and Fridays, which
were fast days.[8]

The main meal was to comprise two cooked dishes, with the addition of fresh vegetables and fruit as a third. In medieval accounts
these are usually referred to as 'pulses', or 'pottage', a soup flavoured with vegetables and herbs and sometimes thickened with
oatmeal. The two dishes were probably originally intended as alternatives, but became instead two courses; we know that this was the
case by about 1100, but in all likelihood the change occurred long
before that. On days when an evening meal was allowed, one-third
of this was supposed to be served then, which probably means that
the meal itself was a cold snack. Bread was provided in addition
to the cooked dishes – as Walter Daniel observed, a pound loaf for
each monk. In Cistercian monasteries, the bread had to be 'coarse',
in other words made of bran or rye rather than refined flour; white
bread could only be served to guests. Since the monastic day was
regulated by the 'offices' – the liturgical hours – monks woke in
what we would consider the middle of the night, for Matins, and
had to be in the church again at about 6 a.m. The main meal was
probably served at about 11.30 or noon, and the evening meal in the
late afternoon, before Vespers. This left a very long gap in which
no food at all – in theory – was available.

Monks knew what they were due, because the *Rule* specified it
so clearly. When they didn't get it, they naturally complained. At
Evesham Abbey in the 1190s and early 1200s, if the chronicler of
Evesham is to be believed, Abbot Roger de Norrys was rather too
vigorous in his interpretation of the *Rule* when it came to diet. For
many days, the chronicler complains, we lived off bread and water
alone, and for many more we had beer that was scarcely better
than water, with no pittances. This was an even worse allocation
of food than that specified as a punishment for rebellious monks
of Whitby in 1287, who were limited to bread, pottage, ale and one
ferculum for four weeks, then bread and water for a further week.

Was Roger simply a zealous abbot trying to enforce the *Rule* on a community that had become too lax? After several years of putting up with him, the monks finally, in 1213, laid their grievances before the papal legate: the abbot regularly failed to provide their statutory dish of beans and there was no beer; the bread was so awful that even the abbot's servants refused it; the meals were served at irregular times and were poorly co-ordinated, so that only rarely were bread, pulses and beer all served together at the same meal; and, moreover, in winter there was sometimes no food at all until Vespers. Not surprisingly, the chronicler complains, some monks and abbey servants died of starvation.[9]

Benedict had left the choice of food – as long as it did not include the meat of a quadruped – to the discretion of individual abbots and cellarers. This was only sensible, for the most plentiful and easily available foods would not be the same everywhere. In the Byzantine world, however, the regulation of food was different. Here, there was no standard formula such as the *Rule of Benedict*; since founders were responsible for regulating monasteries, there could be as many different Rules as there were monasteries.

From the ninth century onward, an increasing number of typika (rules to be followed for daily life) survive from monasteries in the Byzantine Empire. Some prescribe the food to be eaten in precise detail. The basic diet comprised bread, boiled green vegetables, pulses such as lentils and beans, cheese and eggs. Some fish was also eaten when available, usually in the form of a soup. Fresh fruit in season, and dried fruit out of season, were taken as dessert. The beans, lentils or chickpeas were usually made into a thick stew, flavoured with herbs or root vegetables such as onion or leek, and dressed with oil. This is basically the same as the Egyptian dish *ful medames*. It might be made as a thick soup or a stew, depending on the amount and type of pulses used, and it formed the standard monastic dish throughout the Greek Orthodox world in the Middle Ages. Sometimes the soup of stewed onions and herbs was poured over bread. This seems to be something rather different from the delicious Tuscan *zuppe di pane*, in which bread forms one of the principal ingredients of the soup itself. Garlic probably also formed a staple of this kind of dish, even as far away from the Mediterranean as England, where copious quantities of garlic seem to have been grown in monastic gardens. Remarkably, the basic diet of monks in the Greek Orthodox world appears largely unchanged even today. Visiting the monastery of St John on the island of Patmos in 2006, I was able to see the refectory, which is painted with twelfth-century frescoes, laid out for the midday meal. Baskets of fresh fruit and bread were already on the table, and dishes of what looked like a cooked vegetable stew or thick soup were being brought in. The individual places

Orthodox monks' stew

Allow about 35 grams of dried chickpeas per monk. Prepare chickpeas by soaking them in cold water for 8 hours or overnight. (A cellarer who knows his job will ensure that a good supply of dried legumes is kept soaking daily for use the next day, but you can use ready-cooked chickpeas if needed.) If you are using them dried, change the water and bring the chickpeas to the boil over high heat. Cook rapidly for about 10 minutes, then reduce the heat and allow to simmer for another 20 minutes. They should be soft inside but still retain their crunch. Meanwhile, heat some olive or sesame oil in a large saucepan and add four chopped leeks and a sprinkle of oregano; sauté gently. When the chickpeas are cooked, partly drain, reserving about a cupful of water, and add to the saucepan with the leeks; stir gently. Add three whole peeled cloves of garlic, salt and pepper to taste and a teaspoon of cumin. Take a handful of mixed herbs, either basil and thyme or mint; tear roughly and stir into the pot. Sprinkle the top with grated sheep's cheese and put in the oven for 15 minutes, then serve. Alternatively, omit the sheep's cheese, leave to cool and eat cold, with cubes of feta mixed in.

were laid with a certain idiosyncracy, perhaps to take account of some monks' specific dietary needs. The whole arrangement was not unlike the senior common room of an Oxford or Cambridge college – though without the comfortable upholstered furniture.

Since in most of Europe throughout the Middle Ages and well beyond, the basic diet of rural people was dominated by pulses and vegetables of the allium family, it is not surprising that these, together with local herbs and greens, probably featured heavily in monastic refectories. The main principle to be observed in monasteries, according to both Benedict's *Rule* and most Byzantine typika, was that no more than two dishes should be provided for the community at any one meal; so, if lentil stew comprised one dish, the second might be vegetables such as braised cabbage or leeks. The English Benedictine Statutes of 1343 reminded monastery cooks to supply at least two different dishes, so that monks who did not like one dish could make their meal from the other, and 'since sameness in food leads to fussiness'. Bread was supplementary, but that too was fixed by measure – a pound a day for each monk in Benedict's *Rule*, or a single small loaf in the Byzantine world. Monks who had been engaged in manual labour might, at the abbot's discretion, be given more to eat than those who had worked at less arduous tasks. In the East as in the West, two meals were provided daily, not counting breakfast, which usually comprised simply bread and either ale or wine.

Some Greek Orthodox monastic typika prescribed exact amounts of food for each monk. A monastery founded on the Black Mountain near Antioch in the eleventh century is a good example. A measure of rice and one of boiled lentils, beans or chickpeas was to be served to each monk daily – the measure being the equivalent of a serving of wine. This typikon distinguished between cooking the pulses as a stew or in a soup, for the latter of which the proportion of beans to water was less. If the pulses were cooked in the form of a soup, only half a measure was to be used. This might then mean that half a measure could be used for the second meal of the day in some other form. Each monk also had the right to a daily heaped serving of olives, a level serving of raisins, a portion of figs and six nuts. When fresh fruit was available, this system of measures was abandoned for these.

Besides these regulations with regard to quantity, the author of the typikon, Nikon, also specified what kinds of food were to be eaten each day. On Tuesday and Thursday, the menu was soup, vegetables – boiled but not dressed with olive oil – and cheese, eggs and fish if available. These were the days of relative plenty. Mondays, Wednesdays and Fridays, in contrast, were semi-fast days. The monks' fare was restricted to a single vegetable dish without oil, and a dish of dry food such as bread and dried fruit. On Sundays, dishes at both meals were prepared with olive oil. This was the rule until Lent. After the second week of Lent, however, no cooked food at all was to be prepared on weekdays, and the monks had to be content with bread, fruit, olives and whatever vegetables or herbs could be eaten raw.[10]

Most reform-minded founders and regulators took pains to insist that all monks should eat the same food. Neophytos the Recluse, the founder of a rather odd monastery called the Enkleistra, over which he presided from a cell which he never left, ruled that the monks should eat together, and that there should be no complaints about the food. The concern over grumbling about the food seems to have been common across the monastic world: Neophytos' contemporary in England, Abbot Samson of Bury St Edmunds, also took his monks to task for complaining about the food and asking for it to be changed. At the Enkleistra, only the abbot, who was always to be a recluse, was to eat his meagre meal alone. Neophytos himself had reason to complain that on more than one occasion he was forgotten by the rest of the community on a feast day, and because he could not leave his cell, had to go without any food.[11] However, in Benedictine monasteries, as we shall see in the next chapter, it became common for abbots to keep a separate table at which they could entertain guests, and separate food was served here. A twelfth-century Byzantine satiric poem contrasts the food prepared for the rank-and-file monks with that for abbots. This poem provides a jaundiced view of how the basic monastic bean soup or stew was prepared: the cooks filled a four-gallon cauldron with water and threw in pre-soaked beans, twenty onions, some twigs of savory to season it and three splashes of oil. This 'holy soup' was poured over pieces of bread. Meanwhile, the abbot was fasting, as always on Wednesdays and Fridays: no fish for his table, but only lobsters, crabs, stewed crayfish, fried prawns, oysters, clams and mussels, and of course a few green vegetables and lentils to go with them. Beans, too, and peas, rice – with honey – olives, as always, and caviar (fish eggs, after all, are not the same as fish). Fruit finished the abbatial meal: sweet small apples, dates, dried figs, fresh walnuts, raisins and some lemon preserve. As a satire, of course this poem intentionally exaggerates, but in reproducing a list of what was probably presented at aristocratic tables during an official period of fasting, the author reminds his audience that most monasteries were headed by members of the upper classes.[12]

Not all monasteries were run on such lax lines as this poet imagined, even when members of the imperial family were present. It was not uncommon for monasteries to count among their number such dignitaries. Deposition of emperors was not uncommon, and the standard punishment for a deposed emperor and any relatives who might prove troublesome to the new regime was to banish them to a monastery – often after the suitably degrading humiliation of blinding. In the tenth century, Emperor Romanus Lacapenus was deposed by his sons and forced into a monastery, to be followed only a few years later by the same sons, who had themselves fallen victim to the same fate. According to the Italian observer Liutprand of Cremona, when the sons arrived ex-Emperor Romanus greeted them ironically with details of the luxuries on the menu: boiled water served 'colder than the Gothic snow', soft broad beans, green leaves and fresh leeks. 'There are no fishmonger's delicacies to make us ill; but we fall ill instead as a result of the frequent fasting.' Sabas or Nikon themselves would have approved – of the diet, at least, if not of the complaint. The twelfth-century chronicler Anna Komnena bears out the substance of this story when she reports that Emperor Nikephoros Botaneiates, who was deposed in 1081 by Anna's father, Alexios, and exiled to a monastery, regretted only that he missed eating meat.[13]

LENTEN FOOD, AND OTHER FASTS

Those Byzantine monastic typika that expressed an interest in food were particularly concerned that Lenten observances should be clearly specified. Indeed, it is from the Lenten food that we get our clearest picture of how Orthodox monks ate. At the eleventh-century Constantinopolitan monastery of Theotokos Evergetis, for instance, we know that during most of the year breakfast and lunch were the main meals, and that supper, which comprised only bread, a little wine and small fruit, was optional. For Lent, however, we have a much fuller picture of the meals. On the Monday of the first week in Lent, total abstinence was observed – the monks were to eat nothing at all. Between Tuesday and Friday of the first week, monks ate boiled lentils or beans accompanied only by raw vegetables. On the Friday, two cooked dishes were prepared, but without the use of olive oil either in the cooking or as a dressing. On Saturday and Sunday, the two cooked dishes could be dressed with oil. During the rest of Lent, on each Wednesday, the monks could eat the same as on the weekends, but on Tuesdays and

Dried-fruit salad

For winter months, when fresh fruit is hard to come by.

Soak a selection of dried figs, dates, raisins and apricots in water for about 25 minutes, until they are plump and juicy. Drain, chop larger fruit into small chunks and put into a large bowl; add two or three tablespoons of orange juice, and mix. Sprinkle half a teaspoon of ground cloves and tear a few fresh mint leaves over the fruit.

Thursdays olive oil was permitted in only one of the cooked dishes. On Mondays and Fridays, the only food available was plain boiled beans, small fruit and water. On Good Friday, only uncooked food was permissible.[14]

At the Monastery of Makhairas in Cyprus, a thirteenth-century foundation, the Lenten fare comprised lentils or beans with raw vegetables and fruit on Tuesdays, Wednesdays and Thursdays. On Fridays, cooked dishes might be prepared, but sesame oil replaced olive as a form of abstinence. On Saturdays and Sundays, three cooked dishes could be served. During the fast of Holy Apostles at the laura of Athanasius on Mt Athos, fish was reserved for Sundays alone, and olive oil and wine were served only on Tuesdays and Thursdays. Some Western reforming monasteries fasted weekly. At Jubin, a reforming monastery near Antioch founded by Franks, who had come to the East in the wake of the Crusades, the monks ate only bread and water three times a week; on the other days they could eat stewed vegetables, and, very rarely, fish.

There were also stipulations for feast days. On Annunciation Day, the monks of Evergetis were encouraged to eat as splendidly as possible, and to include fish in particular. Monks of the laura of Athanasius ate two cooked dishes daily between Easter and All Saints Day, which had to include garden vegetables and beans with olive oil. On holy days, an extra cooked dish, dressed with oil, was served, and when they were available, fish, cheese and eggs. Outside Lent, cheese and milk were added to the staple pulse and vegetable diet of the monks of Makhairas. This seems to have been the norm in monasteries whose customs derived from the Palestinian tradition of St Sabas.[15]

Individual monks might, with permission, make alterations to the diet, but only in order to observe a more rigorous regime. One of the followers of St Romuald, Gaudentius, asked permission to decline the normal dishes provided and instead to eat only bread, water, apples and raw vegetables. Initially Romuald allowed this, but then changed his mind out of concern for Gaudentius' ability to withstand such rigours. Founders of communities, of course, were free to do as they pleased. A monk from Asia Minor, Lazaros, abstained from wine, olive oil and cheese while living as a monk at St Sabas in the Judaean desert. After founding his first community on Mt Galesion in western Asia Minor – where he lived on a pillar overlooking his monks who occupied cells at ground level – he ate only raw food every Wednesday and Friday. During the three forty-day fasts of Lent, Holy Apostles and Advent, he apparently ate only at weekends. In his final years, he relented to the extent of accepting cooked food daily, but without olive oil. He even drank specially prepared possets for his throat – which had probably suffered from years of haranguing his monks from a great height. In the Western reforming tradition there was broad agreement, but local differences, about what constituted fasting. Peter Damian specified that fasting meant eating only bread, salt and water – Anthony's staple in the Egyptian desert.[16]

OLIVES

No food is more characteristic of the Near East than the olive. Olive cultivation, as anthropologists have argued, marks the boundary between the desert and 'civilized' habitation. Olives have been eaten in the eastern Mediterranean as long as people have lived there. Lawrence Durrell's panegyric to the olive in *Prospero's Cell* captures the meaning of the olive: 'the whole of the Mediterranean . . . seems to rise in the sour, pungent taste of black olives between the teeth. A taste older than meat, than wine.'[17] More prosaically, archaeological excavations have discovered evidence of olive cultivation going back as far as 3000 BC in the region of Jericho, the town that stands by the Jordan on the very edge of the fertile crescent. Wild olives (oleasters) were growing before this, perhaps as early as 8000 BC, but the fruit of the oleaster, while edible, is bitter and the stone is too large in relation to the flesh. At some point, therefore, primitive peoples learned how to cultivate olives that could not only provide a source of food in their raw state, but, more important, oil for cooking and fuel. Olive cultivation and technology spread from Palestine and Syria to Asia Minor, Greece and Crete, and thence, through trade and in the wake of the movement of peoples, to the western Mediterranean: Italy, Spain, southern France and North Africa. In ancient Greek society, the olive came to have a deep cultural, even religious significance. The citizens of Athens developed the tradition that the first olive trees had been given to them as a gift by the goddess Athena, the patron of their city. Destruction of olive trees, which accompanied war between Greek city states, was regarded as a sacrilege as well as an economic threat.

Olive trees can live for many hundreds of years, perhaps even thousands. The few olive trees that one can still see in the Garden of Gethsemane, at the foot of the Mount of Olives, may be about seven hundred years old. But it is notoriously difficult to judge the age of an olive tree because the roots throw out new shoots for hundreds of years, so even when the original tree dies and has to be chopped down, another is likely to grow up from a new set of roots growing on the old stock. For this reason, olive groves themselves can be thousands, rather than hundreds of years old. Another reason why olives have remained such a productive part of the agricultural economy of the Mediterranean is that besides their longevity, they are supremely adaptable plants. Mature olive trees need little pruning or fertilisation, and can manage with very little water. They also stand up well to grafting. There are many techniques for this, but essentially it is possible, by cutting slots in an old branch and inserting into them the tips of younger shoots, to ensure new young growth on an ancient tree. In Palestine, and doubtless elsewhere around the Mediterranean, the same techniques are used to do this as described by the Roman writer Cato in his book *On Farming* in c.175 BC (in which olives receive more attention than any other plant).

Olive oil was indispensable for any monastic community in the ancient or medieval Mediterranean. It was used as a fat for cooking, for dressing vegetables and bread, but most of all as a fuel. Churches needed light, and in the Mediterranean this was easier to obtain from oil lamps, the traditional form of domestic lighting for centuries, than from candles. The multiple liturgical offices in a monastery's church meant the consumption of oil on a large scale. Centuries before Christian monasteries were founded in Palestine, mass production of oil was already well advanced. The Philistine capital, Ekron, exported olive oil to Egypt, Crete and the Greek islands. Archaeologists estimate that Ekron had over a hundred working mills, each producing between seven and ten tons of oil from the annual harvest. A monastery did not need nearly as much as this, but if it wanted to provide for its own needs rather than buying oil, it had to have very large olive orchards. A good olive tree in Beit Jallah, a village near Bethlehem that is considered by many to produce the best olives in Palestine, can produce about eighty or ninety kilos of fruit every year. Five kilos of fruit can yield a bare litre of oil, so a productive tree would only give sixteen or so litres.

The technology for extracting oil from fruit is relatively simple. Olive presses dating back over two thousand years have been found on various Mediterranean archaeological sites. Perhaps more pertinently, they have also been found on village farms in the Holy Land from the Middle Ages that are known to have been parts of the landed property of prominent monasteries. It is evident that olive farming was part of the economy of monasteries in the Near East. First, the fruit must be picked by one of two methods: hand-picking, which is still favoured in the Near East, and which, although labour-intensive, ensures that the fruit-bearing tips remain undamaged; or beating the branches until the fruit falls. Once the fruit is gathered, it must be crushed with the stones intact; it is then separated from the stones, spread on mats and pressed. The resulting fluid separates into oil and a vegetable resin known to the Romans as *amurca*, which is bitter and watery. Modern industrial processes use water to help the separation, but the traditional method used a dry milling process. The oil is then left to sit for several months. All this could be accomplished by cenobitic monasteries, which had reserves of manpower for agricultural work. As well as using olive oil for lamps, monks also ate the fruit. Olives are mentioned as one of the food types in regular use in Pachomius' monasteries in Egypt, and they feature in the menus of Byzantine monasteries in the Middle Ages. To be eaten at their best, olives should be cracked, soaked in water for a few days so that the flesh expands, and cured in more water with salt and lemon juice. The taste of the olives will depend on how long they are left to cure: the longer they are left, the chewier and sweeter they will be.

Olives were so indispensable a part of the Mediterranean diet that several recipes for serving them survive in Byzantine sources, notably in Simeon Seth's dietary treatise. They might be cured in salt, preserved in vinegar or brine, or marinated in vinegar sweetened with honey.

BEANS

Aside from bread, the single most commonly eaten food type in monasteries was probably the bean. Broad beans have been cultivated for millennia in the Middle East, and are still the staple source of protein in Egypt today. In some medieval cultures, a link between the broad bean and the afterlife persisted – doubtless a remnant of ancient Pythagorean ideas that the soul migrated after death into beans. A sixteenth-century Italian church council prohibited the relatives of the deceased from handing out beans to bystanders in church at funerals.

Mention is also made in monastic sources of lentils, chickpeas and red beans, all of which were treated in the same ways: either boiled and dressed with oil, or stewed with fresh vegetables such as onions and herbs. The type of pulse would depend on the region, but beans, lentils and peas were grown all over Europe. After c.AD 1000, productive cultivation of beans increased significantly as result of new agricultural developments. In particular, the invention of the deep-share plough enabled a greater depth of soil to be dug, which in turn allowed for greater productivity.

The ubiquity and also the monotony of pulses in the monastic diet is well illustrated by comparing two anecdotes, one from sixth-century Palestine, the other from twelfth-century Burgundy. In the first, which we have already seen, Sabas teaches the monk James a lesson by serving him leftover beans dried in the sun and recooked. There is also a story about peas in a collection of miracles told by the Cistercian monk Herbert of Clairvaux in the later twelfth century. In this *exemplum*, or moral story, a novice at Clairvaux was struggling with his vocation. As he told his abbot, he found many things about the Cistercian way of life too difficult, but worst of all was the quality and monotony of the diet. He felt he simply could not bear another meal consisting of beans or peas. Now the novice is described as a rather soft and cosseted young man, and the abbot evidently made allowances for both his youth and the habits of his upbringing. The abbot persuaded the young

Clairvaux 'miracle peas'

This recipe is inspired by the story told in Herbert of Clairvaux's *Book of Miracles* about a Cistercian novice who became so fed up with the food at Clairvaux that only by a miracle could he be induced to carry on eating split peas. You will probably need to use quorn bacon to produce your miracle. Begin by soaking yellow split peas overnight in cold water. Rinse and drain in fresh cold water, put in a large saucepan and cover with salted water; bring this to the boil rapidly. After about 10 minutes of boiling, reduce heat, skim off the surface, cover and simmer for another 20 minutes, until peas are soft and beginning to fall apart. Meanwhile, cut quorn bacon into very small cubes and fry in a little oil with two cloves of crushed garlic. Drain the peas, retaining a very small amount of the liquid, and return to the saucepan. Stir in the quorn bacon and garlic, add a little more salt if needed, and tear some fresh mint, thyme and basil leaves into the pot. At the final stage, you can leave out the bacon, and simply pour over the peas the garlic and oil in which it has cooked.

man to stick it out for three more days. At dinner that same day, the novice sat down in the refectory to be confronted by the usual daily bowl of split peas. Instantly he regretted this decision, telling himself he should have left immediately. So disgusted was he by the peas that he thought he would retch, but he forced himself to take a mouthful. To his astonishment, this time, he found the dish richer in flavour even than meat, and finished it greedily. Suspecting that the abbot had ordered his dish to be flavoured specially with lard or bacon as a ruse to keep him in the monastery, he went to the kitchen to interrogate the cook. The abbot, cook and serving boys all denied that anything other than salt and water had gone into the dish. The novice then realized that God was able to imbue simple pulses and greens with the same flavour that one associates with meat and fish. For one monk at least, the key to the monastic diet was imagination and the power of suggestion.[18]

FISH

Fish offered considerable advantages for religious communities and individual hermits. For one thing, it was – or could be – free for those who lived close enough to freshwater rivers or the sea and who could organize means of catching it. For another, it was thought by some to be a particularly virtuous food to eat. Jesus' apostles had been fishermen, and there was a view that because of this, fish was as close as one could attain on earth to the food on the menu in heaven. Certainly fishing was regarded as the only legitimate form of hunting for monks and clergy.

Some of the Byzantine typika permit fish to be eaten on certain days, but there seems to have been little pattern to fish-eating. The availability of fish and shellfish obviously depended on the season and the closeness of the monastery either to a fish market or to the coast or a river. Thus the nuns serving the tomb of the Empress Irene Douka (founded in Constantinople in 1118) ate fish on most days of the week, and shellfish – considered less grand a food – on Tuesdays. The monastery of Pantokrator in Constantinople (founded in 1136) provided for shellfish and oysters on Mondays, and permitted either salted or fresh fish on any other day except Wednesday, which was a fast day. Constantinople was a fishing port as well and had a plentiful market, and fish may have been as easy to obtain as fresh vegetables. However, a fifteenth-century traveller, Pero Tafur, thought that shellfish were eaten so often in monasteries during Lent because they were regarded as 'bloodless' and therefore more appropriate to fasting.[19]

Fish also appears on the monastic table through serendipity, often as a result of a personal gift. Thus the Evergetis typikon allows fish if provided by a guest. Solitary monks seem not to have put much effort into catching fish for themselves, or at least the hagiographical sources do not indicate so. This may seem surprising, given the opportunities for solitary contemplation offered by fishing, but perhaps hagiographers did not want to give the impression that their subjects devoted inordinate amounts of time to pursuits other than devotions. Or perhaps they did not need to fish themselves in order to enjoy eating it. The English hermit Godric of Finchale provided a salmon through miraculous intervention, when unexpected guests from Durham Cathedral Priory turned up. He sent his understandably sceptical servant to the stream, ignoring the boy's protestations that it was high summer and that the stream was dry. It was indeed summer, Godric replied; the feast of St John the Baptist, and the saint will not allow our guests to go unfed. The boy grumbled but went anyway, and duly returned with a huge salmon.[20] Similarly, the monks of Clairvaux fed the pope with an unexpectedly caught fish, when it appeared that the food that had been prepared for the papal entourage was not enough to go round. In another example of the theme, Peter Damian tells the story of how the visit of a great hermit, Romuald, to Sitria prompted a miraculous catch of fish from a river that was normally unpopulated. Clearly, the symbolism of these unexpected catches of fish echoes the Gospel story of the miraculous draught on the Sea of Galilee. Many monasteries in fact farmed their own fish in purpose-built ponds, some of which can still be seen in the contours of surviving monastic ruins, and river fisheries are also described in the charters of some monasteries.

The relationship between permitted fish and banned meat clearly caught the attention of contemporaries. In one intriguing anecdote, Francis of Assisi was once given a fat capon to share with his followers. Taking the same view of this as Hilarion's bishop, they sat down to eat. As they did so, a beggar came by to plead for some of the food, and was invited to dine with the friars. Next day, the ungrateful man publicly denounced Francis for eating meat, and produced the remains of the capon as evidence. As he showed it, however, he saw that it had miraculously turned into the skeleton of a fish, thus clearing Francis' reputation.[21] This story indicates that although Francis thought it acceptable to eat meat when it was given to him, the basic principle that men of God did not eat flesh was deep-rooted in society. Some twelfth-century monastic reformers thought, as Francis later would, that hermits who needed to survive at least in part on alms could not afford to be too choosy about their diet, and should eat whatever they were given, even if that included meat. John Gualbert, an eleventh-century Italian monk who founded an influential reform monastery at Vallombrosa, allowed his monks to eat meat if nothing else were available. This principle seems to have been adopted by English monasteries in the later Middle Ages. The King's Articles of 1421 – a set of regulations for monastic observance in the province of Canterbury – allowed monasteries to serve meaty foods as substitutes for fish on fast days in regions where a regular supply of fish could not be assured. Tripe and sausages are specified as legitimate substitutes in such cases.

The kinds of fish eaten varied depending on availability. England had well-established herring fisheries in the North Sea and English Channel, but most fishing was probably in-shore or estuary until the development of purpose-built fish ponds from the twelfth century onwards. Even then, monastic taste seems to have been for saltwater fish rather than freshwater. Given this, a good deal of the fish eaten in monasteries in Europe was probably preserved rather than fresh: herring or stockfish (dried cod) were very widespread, but haddock, ling, hake and conger eel has also been identified by zooarchaeologists on monastic sites. Herring seems to have swamped the market in the later Middle Ages, perhaps because of the development of the herring fisheries and herring trade in the North Sea, but also because of the ease with which it can be preserved and thus brought inland. Excavations at Eynsham Abbey in Oxfordshire, which is not close to any source of fresh saltwater fish, have yielded huge numbers of herring bones, most of which can be identified as having come from preserved rather than fresh fish because of the absence of head bones. Although it is impossible to estimate how much fish was eaten in monasteries, bone deposits

Fish and herbs

The kind of fish you use will depend on what has been caught or provided by a guest to the monastery. Supposing you have two large or three or four smaller fish, cut off the heads and fillet the fish. Put heads and bones in a small pot, cover with water and add salt, pepper and a bay leaf; bring to the boil rapidly, then simmer for 25 minutes. Meanwhile, place fillets in a baking dish in half an inch of water or milk; bake in a medium oven for 15–20 minutes. Remove and allow to cool, then either cut the fish into chunks or flake carefully. Meanwhile chop and sauté a large onion in oil in a wide-bottomed saucepan; when the onion is translucent, add a chopped green pepper. After a few minutes, tip the fish into the pan and stir gently, trying not to break the fish pieces. Add the stock from the fish heads and simmer gently. Meanwhile, wash and chop a couple of handfuls of wild herbs, preferably including wild fennel and either fat hen or, if you are near a coastline, sea beet. Stir these into the pan, cover and leave to cook for 10 minutes. This dish is excellent poured over thick slices of toast that have been rubbed with a clove of garlic.

can help to reconstruct ratios of different foods. At St Gregory's Priory in Canterbury, nine times as many fish bones have been excavated as bird bones; this compares with a ratio of three to two from the royal manor of Hextalls in Surrey.

Fish ponds were popular among those who could afford to dig and maintain them from the twelfth century onwards. The obvious advantage that they offered was freedom from competition with other landowners, such as is frequently recorded over fishing rights on stretches of river and lakes. Ponds are found in England and France, and there is plenty of evidence from both archaeology and documentary sources of their extent and the expense of keeping them up. However, they were worth the expense because of the variety of piscine diet they offered — pike, bream, roach and eels, for example. Naturally, having fish ponds lessened a monastery's dependence on buying in fish, which for inland monasteries usually meant eating preserved rather than fresh. Monasteries that could afford it invested in substantial buildings associated with fish ponds. A surviving example is the fourteenth-century fish house built by the abbot of Glastonbury at Meare in Somerset, a two-storey building next to the fish ponds and a larger lake. Such a building may well indicate that some processing of fish also went on there, which in turn suggests that some of the monastery's fish was sold on the open market.

CHEESE AND DAIRIES

Milk, cheese and butter were all popular in the refectory in both the Mediterranean and Western Europe for a variety of reasons. The cheeses mentioned in sources describing eastern Mediterranean monasticism were probably mostly made from goats' or sheep's milk, though there is also evidence of buffalo being kept for milk. The simplest cheese was a curd made from the fermented milk and moulded into balls or small cakes, probably similar to Greek feta. Easting cheese took on theological importance in Orthodox monasteries influenced by the Palestinian tradition. The typikon of the

Black Mountain, for instance, insists that cheese should be on the menu in the first weeks of Lent 'to combat the Armenian heresy'. This refers to a custom followed by Armenians in which the whole of Lent was a time of complete abstinence from all dairy products. But the custom among some extreme reformers in the West was to eschew cheese, milk and eggs altogether, as, for example, among the hermits described by Gerard of Nazareth in the Holy Land in the mid-twelfth century.

In contrast, cheese and dairy products were a standard part of monastic fare in Western Europe. Monks ate large numbers of eggs, but in this they were probably following the standard diet of upper-class society. In 1491–2, over 80,000 eggs were bought by Westminster Abbey over a period of some thirty-two weeks, which works out, Barbara Harvey suggests, to about five eggs per monk daily. These would have been eaten in various forms, of course: flans, puddings, omelettes and custards. A rich cheese flan was especially popular during May. Outside Lent, the monks probably also ate cheese on its own, particularly at supper.

Cheese making traditionally ran from April or May to October, because these are the months when milk-producing animals – especially sheep and goats – are lactating the most. A longer season is possible for cows, especially if they can be fed all year round. Some monasteries earned a reputation for high-quality cheese production. Llanthony Priory in the Black Mountains of Wales, which Gerald of Wales had in the twelfth century praised as a miracle of land management, made a cheese celebrated throughout England. Monastic cheese was also exported. For example, Ogbourne Priory, a dependent cell of Bec in Normandy, was required to send thirty-two weys a year to the mother-house – this amounted to an enormous 5,760 pounds. We can trace the production of dairy goods in a typical English Cistercian abbey in the thirteenth century. Beaulieu Abbey in Hampshire produced cheese in its granges in the New Forest for consumption at the monastery. In 1269–70, the total amount of cheese recorded as having been received by the cellarer was 65 weys (11,700 pounds). Typically, this was sheep's cheese rather than cows' or goats'. However, of this total, only a small proportion (3,328 pounds) was eaten in the form of cheese itself. Some was used in cooking pottage, but a large amount, some 15 per cent, was recorded as waste because it had dried out and was inedible.[22] One hundred and forty men (about half of whom were monks and the other half lay brothers) were to be fed by these amounts. This means that each monk had a ration of not much more than 2¼ ounces of cheese, if we take out days on which cheese couldn't be eaten because of fasting rules. It looks as though Cistercian monasteries remained quite strict in their observance of the *Rule*, at least in the later thirteenth century. But even at Westminster in the fifteenth century, cheese eating was quite restrained, and probably amounted to not much more than 2½ ounces per day.

MEDIEVAL HERMITS AND SOLITARIES

The Cistercians were the most successful of the groups of monks in twelfth-century Europe who were influenced by the ideal of 'returning to the desert'. Although they lived cenobitically, the early Cistercians thought of themselves as hermits. In an intriguing passage in William of St Thierry's reminiscences of Clairvaux, he describes the monks as living eremitical lives even though they are members of a community.[23] Does he mean that they are eremitical in the original sense of the word *eremum* ('wilderness')? Or that they live, even communally, in conscious imitation of the desert fathers in terms of ascetic conduct? At any rate, the later eleventh and first half of the twelfth centuries saw a remarkable fluidity between the states of solitary and communal monasticism. Some monks left their monasteries to go and live as hermits in the wilderness, often founding new communities as like-minded people followed them; others fluctuated between periods of solitary and communal living; while still others abandoned safe berths as cathedral canons or parish clergy to become solitaries. The boundaries between the categories of religious living that had seemed so secure to John Cassian in the early fifth century were much more difficult to define in the twelfth. The process of abandoning a settled career in the Church in order to become a hermit entailed dealing in some way with the business of feeding oneself. Robert of Arbrissel, an influential reforming canon in northwest France in the late eleventh century, threw up a promising career in the Church in favour of a wandering ministry. Eventually he founded the reforming house of Fontevrault in Anjou, where he specialized in taking in abandoned women who had been forced to turn to prostitution. Before this, however, he lived as a hermit in the forests of Brittany, surviving – like a pig, according to his first biographer – on acorns, nuts and roots. A slightly later biographer, in more reasoned fashion, claimed that it was while living in the woods that Robert learned to eat only boiled herbs and water – like John the Baptist, as he remarked.[24]

Surviving on what one can find in the wild has of course been a way of life for hunter-gatherer peoples throughout history, and even in settled societies the poor have always known how to use 'free food' to supplement their diet. But the eleventh and twelfth centuries saw a large number of men (and some women) consciously abandon settled lives as part of a movement of religious revival in order to embrace poverty. They chose to live on the margins of society, in the knowledge that their ability to survive would depend in large measure on their ability to find food. A good example of the phenomenon is the career of Stephen of Obazine. Stephen, a native of western France, went off to become a solitary monk with only a single companion. They camped in the dense ancient woodlands of the Limousin region. During their first winter in the woods, they almost starved, and were only saved by a neighbouring peasant woman who brought them some bread and milk. Once they had been discovered and identified as holy men, Stephen and his companion were kept alive by the neighbouring peasant communities, until their pitch was queered by the arrival of a charlatan who set himself up as a hermit in the same forest, and accepted gifts of food and clothing from the local people on the promise of saying Mass for them – yet, when they went to his hut to hear the Mass, they found he had run away with their gifts. After that, Stephen was thrown on the resources of the forest. He and his companion were reduced to digging up roots and even stripping bark from the trees to eat. They evidently found 'grazing' more difficult than their Syrian and Palestinian predecessors had done. This was doubtless partly a matter of experience and local knowledge, but also of timing: had they chosen to settle in the woods in the spring or summer, they could have had their pick of wild herbs, fruit and berries. Bernard of Tiron, while living as a hermit in the forest of Craon before founding the reform monastery that bore his name, found a honeycomb that kept him alive for some time.[25]

The reference to tree bark may appear to confirm our suspicions that the author of the *Life of Stephen of Obazine* was using rhetorical licence in order to show how desperately Stephen was in trouble. In fact, tree bark has been eaten by many indigenous peoples. Some native Americans shredded birch bark into strips and boiled it, or dried it and ground it into a flour to make tree-bread. The Zuni, an indigenous Central American people, pounded the inner strips of the pinon tree into a kind of mash, and baked it in the form of cakes in a firepit; before eating, the cakes would then be boiled in water. In Siberia, the Tungens use the bark of the larch to make a kind of broth or tea. Many trees, not only the well-known maple, have a gum or sap that has nutritional value. For example, the birch, pine and hemlock are all rich in natural sugars, and they are indigenous to Europe. Even without the expert knowledge of native customs – and Stephen may have known some local tree lore – it is possible to gain nutrition from tree bark. The *SAS Survival Handbook* lists eleven families of tree considered to have edible bark, and in addition provides instructions for gathering and preparing it. One should apparently choose bark from near the base of the trunk, pull it back to reveal the inner layer, and either chew this raw or, if one has the necessary apparatus, boil it into a gelatinous mass which can be roasted, ground for flour, or used to thicken a stew of edible plants. The eleven edible varieties, apparently, are slippery elm, basswood, birch, aspen, tamarack, poplar, maple, spruce, willow, pine and hemlock. Probably half of these would have been within easy reach of Stephen in the forest of the Limousin in the twelfth century. The twigs of some trees, such as juniper and birch, are also edible. Doughty saw Beduin chewing the twigs of the thaluk bush, together with wild sorrel, but they can also be boiled or simply steeped in hot water to soften them.

Gerard of Nazareth, a twelfth-century bishop in the Frankish Crusader States, penned a series of short portraits of monks he knew who were active in the middle of the century. Among these were solitaries and monks living in reforming communities. One of the most striking features of his account is the way in which Western monks living in the Holy Land revived centuries-old local monastic traditions and practices. One monk, Rainald, used to leave his monastery on Mt Tabor every Lent to live by the banks of the Jordan, taking with him only some bread and a trowel for digging up roots to eat. Did he know that he was copying exactly

Tree bark

Strip off a few good handfuls of bark from near the bottom of one of the following trees: aspen, birch, poplar, slippery elm, maple, spruce, willow or pine. Using a sharp knife, peel back the inner layer from the outer bark, and throw into boiling water. Depending on the type of tree, after about 30 minutes the bark will lose its shape and be reduced to a mash. Add seasoning, and use as a thickener for Hermit's stew [see Chapter 2]. If you cut the bark into thin strips before boiling, the result is not unlike noodles.

Alternatively, when bark has boiled for about 30 minutes, remove from the pot, drain and leave to dry, then sprinkle with salt and place on a baking sheet in a hot oven. After about an hour, the bark can be eaten like a flat bread.

the same custom that had first been introduced by the Palestinian desert fathers Chariton and Euthymius? Another solitary, Bernard of Nazareth, ate only on three days of the week; a monk who looked after lepers in Jerusalem, Alberic, ate only barley bread and water for long periods; Ralph, a pilgrim who stayed in the Holy Land as a hermit, fasted on bread and water three days a week, and even on non-fasting days would not touch eggs or milk, and only rarely ate fish; Henry, however, refused to eat anything that had been killed, including even eggs in this prohibition, but he drank copious quantities of milk.[26]

Eventually, a community was established as word spread far enough to attract followers who wished to join Stephen. Once they had begun to construct a monastery, the tipping point of the new community had been reached. New recruits meant more mouths to feed, but it also meant extra human resources to help gather food, and perhaps expertise in using and preparing wild food. A solitary monk such as Romuald could survive, if he pleased, on beans and boiled chickweed, as Peter Damian reports that he did, but it is more difficult to feed a community on such fare. As Thoreau observed centuries later of his experiences in the wilderness of New England, it is easy enough for a single person to live reasonably well without money if he or she has energy, seeds and a small patch of land to plant them, and sufficient knowledge. Medieval precursors of Thoreau are well attested in the sources: the eleventh-century Greek hermit Luke the Younger cleared a patch of waste land in the Peloponnese to plant a garden, and even fashioned a rough-and-ready mill to grind his own grain – a good system until it was stolen by pirates; Cyril Philoctetes, a Greek hermit in Calabria, grew his own vegetables; Lazaros of Mt Gelasion was given land by the bishop of Ephesos on which to plant beans; and Godric of Finchale planted a vegetable garden near his hermitage in County Durham. His food is described as a stew of vegetables he had grown himself, with wild grasses and herbs. Typically he cooked up large batches of this and kept it for several days, eating a portion of it every evening.

Once Romuald had established a community of like-minded hermits, greater variety and quantities of food were needed, but also the equipment and space to provide such food. The menu was still simple – fish-based soup and vegetables featured heavily – but it required a greater level of organization than had been needed by a single hermit. Similarly, Stephen's community at Obazine probably grew or harvested from the forest most of what they ate, but the process of turning it into food for the monks and nuns – for he also recruited women – required the establishment of a kitchen. Working in the kitchen was regarded as one of the acceptable forms of manual labour in the monastery. According to the *Life of Stephen of Obazine*, the food consisted largely of vegetable soups. While the monastery was in the process of being built, those who were less able to help by quarrying and carrying stone, or in the building work itself, were allowed to prepare the meals, serve and clear up afterwards. Stephen himself helped in this way.

4.   Serving hatch. Tintern Abbey kitchens, Monmouthshire

Obazine eventually became a Cistercian community. Stephen initially resisted the demands of his brethren to adopt a fixed rule, preferring to regulate according to his own instincts – by custom rather than by rule. After his death, however, the community agreed to adopt Cistercian customs, thereby becoming incorporated into the Cistercian association as a daughter-house. During his lifetime, Stephen's preference had been for the adoption of his community by the Carthusians, another of the new monastic orders that made such an impact on religious life in the West in the twelfth century. If the Cistercians came to dominate reform monasticism in Europe, the reform that most closely resembled the practices of the desert fathers was the monastery founded by Bruno of Cologne in the Alps at Chartreuse, near Grenoble. The Carthusians lived in individual cells within a monastic enclosure, meeting only for weekly offices, but otherwise praying, meditating and working alone. In some ways they are the medieval European equivalent of the laura monks of the Holy Land. Food was provided daily for each monk in his cell, as it still is in Carthusian monasteries. The staples are still bread, vegetables and pulses, often cooked as a soup. However, each monk's cell also had a little plot of garden behind it, and here monks could grow their own vegetables and herbs. In the next chapter, we will look at some of the kinds of herbs that monasteries cultivated.

Chapter Four

Herbs and health

In 1142, Bernard of Clairvaux sent a group of his monks to Italy to found a daughter-house not far from Rome. The site chosen was a ruined former Greek Orthodox monastery, St Anastasius, and the leader of the group was an Italian Cistercian who had only recently become a monk at Clairvaux. Three years later, he was to be elected pope as Eugenius III. A letter written by Bernard to the monks paints a vivid picture of the difficulties under which they laboured in founding the new monastery:

> I know that the district in which you live is unhealthy, and that many of you labour under infirmities . . . But not only is it not in agreement with your vow as religious to have recourse to medicines for the body; nor is it really conducive to health. It is certainly permitted to make use sometimes of simples of little value, and this is frequently done. But to purchase drugs, to call in doctors, and to take potions and remedies, this is neither becoming to our vow, nor befits the honour and purity of our order.[1]

Bernard's warning against using doctors is neither as draconian, nor as misanthropic as it may seem. We should not imagine that he wanted his monks to suffer illness, not even as part of their regime of self-denial; rather, avoiding medical practitioners was sometimes sound policy, since outside specialist schools or the courts of the wealthy and powerful, the standard of medicine was low. Although there was a good deal of theoretical knowledge of classical medicine, the relationship between practitioners and the learned was usually slight. The term *medicus* occurs frequently in Italian sources, but in the mid-twelfth century it was only beginning to imply any kind of professional regulation. Much of the practical knowledge of medicine concerned the setting of broken bones and the care of wounds sustained in combat rather than internal medicine. Instead of calling in help that might be of limited use, and buying drugs with unknown provenances, Bernard was recommending that the monks should rely on the methods used by most monasteries for healing the sick, i.e. herbs, or 'simples' made from herbs. After all, Benedict himself had, in his *Rule*, specified that monks should care for the sick. Medieval monasteries throughout Europe were centres of herb cultivation. Indeed, for Bernard to recommend the use of herbs as a vital part of the care for the monks suggests that planting a herb garden was one of the first tasks for the new monastery. Some monastic herb gardens still survive, like that of Westminster Abbey, or have been reconstructed by archaeologists, like that at the Carthusian monastery at Mount Grace in North Yorkshire.

Herbs were grown in medieval monasteries and convents for two main purposes: in kitchen gardens for use in cooking, and in infirmary gardens for use in producing medicines. There was of course considerable overlap between the two, since many herbs were considered to have healing properties in addition to their culinary uses, and in a smaller monastery a single garden served both purposes. A great deal of our knowledge of the kinds of herbs grown in monastery gardens and the purposes for which they were regarded as useful comes from a tradition of writing 'herbals', or treatises about the medicinal properties of herbs.

PLANT LORE IN THE MIDDLE AGES

Ultimately, medieval knowledge of all plants and their properties, including herbs for both eating and healing, came from Aristotle's observation and categorization of natural history in the fourth century BC. Aristotle's pupil at the Academy in Athens, Theophrastus, took his master's work further with his *History of Plants,* a work that seems to have been known equally to educated Romans and scholars in the early Christian period – the 'golden age' of monasticism. It was used heavily by Pliny the Elder, and via Pliny in the earliest encyclopedia in the Western tradition, Isidore of Seville's *Etymologies*, written in the sixth century. Isidore listed 133 herbs, including asphodel, cyclamen, zizania, hyssop, chelidon – and mushrooms!

Aristotelian botany languished for three hundred years before being revived by the Carolingian monk Rabanus Maurus in the ninth century, but the great age of Aristotle in the Middle Ages was the thirteenth century. Whereas earlier Aristotelian scholarship had relied on what little of the great master's work had been translated into Latin, or paraphrased in Latin works such as Pliny's, the new wave of learning came from translations from Arabic. This was because in the early days of Islam, the bulk of the ancient Greek philosophical corpus had been voraciously consumed by Arab scholars. Greek was still unknown to all but a very few scholars in Europe before the fifteenth century, but from about 1100 onwards a number of scholars went to the great centres of learning in Spain, such as Toledo, and employed Mozarabs – Christians brought up in Islamic Spain and who knew Arabic – to make translations of Aristotle from Arabic into Latin.

During the Crusades, a new route became available as some European settlers in the Near East learned Arabic. The compilation of natural history by the Christian Arab Nicholas of Damascus, based heavily on Aristotle, was translated into Latin in the thirteenth century. This work in turn influenced the greatest of all medieval natural historians: the German Dominican scholar Albert 'the Great'. Albert's particular contribution to botany was the thorough classification of plants, made possible by his careful observation of the detailed structures of plants. He had an instinct for morphology, shown, for example, in his recognition that the tendril on a vine was the incomplete development of the fruit. Albert, a theologian, was ultimately interested in theological rather than culinary or medicinal questions prompted by his study of plants. Did plants, given that they were in some sense living things, have anything like a soul? Did plants that existed in a symbiotic relationship – such as when, for example, ivy grew around the trunk of a tree – enjoy a union of any kind? How could species mutate so that a wild plant, when raised domestically, developed different characteristics?

Alongside the academic Aristotelian tradition, and in some cases only partly influenced by it, there were many collections of practical herbal lore. Perhaps the earliest European work dealing with the medicinal properties of plants is the *Materia medica* of the first-century scholar Dioscorides Anazarbeus, which lists and describes about 500 plants. About four hundred years after its first appearance, Dioscorides' *Materia* was copied in a deluxe illuminated manuscript for Juliana Anicia, a member of the imperial ruling family. Largely because of these illustrations, Dioscorides dominated European botanical knowledge until the sixteenth century. Cassiodorus, a contemporary of St Benedict who founded a rather aristocratic and intellectual monastery in southern Italy, recommended Dioscorides' illustrated work for monks who could not read the Greek of Galen or Aristotle but would be able to identify the plants from the pictures.

Around the same time that Juliana Anicia was browsing through her manuscript of Dioscorides, a herbal heavily based on it was probably circulating even more widely. This was the *Herbarium* by Apuleius Platonicus, a more practical, less academic work, designed to list most known herbs with descriptions of their appearance so that they could be easily recognized and of their properties so that they could be used as 'simples', or basic constituents of compound medicines. These descriptions also contain another element that we would probably regard as 'superstition'. There are directions not only for how the plants are to be used, but also for how they are to be picked in the first place. Sometimes these advise, for example, the best time of day for picking, or include verses to be said while picking them. The *Herbarium* was popular throughout the Middle Ages, especially in England: it was translated from Latin into Old English for King Alfred in the early ninth century, and there are also eleventh-century English

manuscripts. Since in that period virtually all manuscript production was done in monasteries, we can infer that the *Herbarium*, and
collections like it, were known and used by monastic communities.
Indeed, monks produced their own herbals. England may have
been more advanced than the continent in this respect, at least
in so far as herbals were produced in the spoken language – Old
English – whereas no other European vernacular could boast the
same. This did not mean, however, that Old English medicine was
cut off from 'learned' writing. The first known Old English medical
text, the *Leech Book of Bald*, dating from the early tenth century, is a
compendium of earlier and current Greek and Latin sources, but
'customized' for use by a monastic community.

Such customization of standard medical or herbal literature was
inevitable given the way books circulated and were produced in the
age before printing. A monastic community that wanted to acquire
a herbal would borrow a manuscript from another monastery and
copy it out. In the process, the monks doing the copying might
make mistakes, or include other material: perhaps local lore known
to them, or anecdotal information from their own experience. In
this way, an eleventh-century manuscript of Apuleius' *Herbarium*
added herbs and herbal remedies to the original without worrying
about the integrity of the original authorship. Manuscripts, unlike
printed books, could also function as commonplace books or
scrapbooks, with the result that bits and pieces of herbals – recipes
or brief descriptions of plants, for example – might be inserted into
odd spare pages in a manuscript among other works of a related,
or even of a completely different, nature. Thus, for example, a
thirteenth-century manuscript from the Benedictine monastery of
St Guthlac at Crowland in Lincolnshire includes a veritable pot-
pourri of different works related to health and healing. It includes
a treatise on the medical care of horses, a pseudo-Aristotelian
treatise and a letter purporting to be by Hippocrates. There are
also random recipes and charms for preparing herbal concoctions.
Each herbal, therefore, was unique to the monastery in which it
was copied.[2]

The invention of print meant that although this organic feature of books was lost, books could be circulated as never before. During the 1480s, both Latin and German herbaria were printed, and 1491 saw the printing of the popular *Hortus Sanitatis*. The German *Herbarium* was clearly the work of a well travelled and cultivated man. He was wealthy enough to pay for an artist to accompany him on his pilgrimage to the Holy Land and Mt Sinai to draw the native herbs and plants that he wanted to include in book – 435 in all. An early French herbal, *Le grant herbier*, survives in two fifteenth-century manuscripts, but was translated into English and printed in English as *The Grete Herball* in 1526.

FOOD VALUES AND HUMOURS

Many of the foods referred to in this book, both those cultivated and growing wild, were eaten by hermits and monks because they were easy to gather or grow, versatile, and simply because they formed part of the staple diet of ordinary people in the regions in question. But monks were also aware of their nutritional values and health-giving properties. Food and medicine were closely linked in the ancient world, and it was from the medical lore of antiquity that medieval medical ideas developed – in particular, theories about food values derived from the writings of the Greek doctor Galen and his followers. Galen (AD 129–99) studied medicine in Alexandria, and developed a reputation in Rome as a surgeon to gladiators. The links between the Coliseum and the imperial court meant that he eventually became the doctor and friend of Emperor Marcus Aurelius. Galen was an advocate of the traditional Greek medical idea, propounded originally by Hippocrates, that the body was made up of a mixture of the four 'humours': black bile, yellow bile, blood and phlegm. Each of these substances governed a particular characteristic temperament and was associated with one of the four elements and with a specific bodily organ. Thus black bile, corresponding to the element earth and to the spleen, produced melancholy; yellow bile, corresponding to fire and located in the gall bladder, led to anger; blood was associated with air and the liver, and produced a sanguine temperament; while phlegm was watery, associated with the brain and lungs, and led to a phlegmatic temperament. Each humour also had properties relating to warmth, cold and so on: yellow bile was warm and dry; black bile, cold and dry; blood, warm and moist; phlegm, cold and moist. Proper health, Galen taught, lay in maintaining a balance between these tendencies. Since some people were predisposed to one or other humour, it was necessary to ensure that the others were compensated for in their intake in order to achieve balance.

The influence of Galen on the medieval understanding of health and diet cannot be underestimated. In Byzantium, Galen's writings provided the material for a series of derivative compilations such as *Peri Trophon Dunameis* ('On the power of foods'). Another derivative treatise by Symeon Seth, 'On Ailments', which links treatments of some maladies to specific foods, became highly influential in its own right in the Greek-speaking world. Symeon Seth was a Jewish physician, probably from the Greek-speaking city of Antioch, who served as palace chamberlain to the Byzantine emperor Michael VII (1071–78). Although Symeon's work takes Galen's theories as a starting point, he also made use of Arabic and Persian medical and dietary texts, and in fact is rather critical of Galen in the light of his knowledge of these Eastern traditions. One feature of the derivative treatises is that their authors had to take account of new foods that were being introduced into Mediterranean markets. For example, when the aubergine appeared from India, via the Arab world, Symeon Seth could not find any vegetable corresponding to it in Galen, and had to use his own experimental knowledge.[3]

Most large monastic libraries probably owned a few such treatises. Indeed some typika, such as Nikon's for the monastery on the Black Mountain, written in the late eleventh century, refer specifically to them in advising on the food regime. A literate hermit or monk would have found guidance here that added a further dimension to the choice of foods available in the typika or recommended by tradition.

Use of Galenic dietary treatises was not confined to the Greek Orthodox world. Summaries of Galen's works and derivative treatises are known to have been made in eleventh-century Italy, and to have been used by some reforming communities in the West. Aelred's monastery of Rievaulx, for example, owned a Latin commentary on Galen made in Italy – probably in the south, where there was a large Greek-speaking population and many Greek monasteries. As a Cistercian monastery founded in the first flush of reformist expansion (1134), Rievaulx followed as far as possible the literal prescriptions of the *Rule of Benedict* in regulating the amount of food served to monks.

Western monks were not reliant simply on translations from the Greek for advice on nutrition and health. Manuals of health based on the judicious use of herbs and other foods were composed and re-drafted in various forms throughout the Middle Ages. Some, such as the *Tacinium Sanitatis,* were copied and illustrated with depictions of herbs and health-giving plants to create a kind of pictorial encyclopedia that was obviously designed for practical use. The *Tacinium* was derived from an Arabic original, the *Taquin as-Sihhah* – the word *Tacinium* coming from the Arabic word for tables, *taqwim* . The author was a Christian Arab, Ibn Butlan, who is known to have worked as a physician in Mosul and Aleppo in the middle of the eleventh century. He eventually became a monk in Antioch, and died in c.1070. Ibn Butlan was himself influenced by the most important Arab earlier medical text, the *Book of Experiences* by Rhazes (869–925), which had emphasized diet in place of medicines as a more holistic and balanced approach to healing. Ibn Butlan argued that sickness came from the disharmony introduced to the body by lack of clean air, overeating, overwork or over-emotive states.

The *Tacinium* may have been translated into Latin as early as the late eleventh century, but the heyday of such translation activities was the twelfth and thirteenth centuries, when Latin-speaking communities were a constant presence in the eastern Mediterranean as a result of the Crusades. A Latin version of the *Tacinium* was made in the reign of King Manfred of Sicily (1254–66), a period when Palermo was a centre of Arabic scholarship. Further Latin translations are known elsewhere in the West in the fourteenth and fifteenth centuries. Since manuscripts were so labour-intensive to produce, we can assume that when a work was copied, it is evidence of demand for it. The *Tacinium*, or works so similar as to be obvious derivations from it, survive in 60 or so manuscripts from the thirteenth century onwards. The reason for its popularity is probably that these manuscripts were all illustrated with a considerable degree of realism. They were intended to be used by herbalists and physicians to recognize plants in their natural state.

A version of the *Tacinium* made in Verona for the bishop of Trento, George of Liechtenstein, in the 1390s, lays out the principles of the book in a preface: 'This is a manual of health that shows those things that should be done by illustrating the positive sides of various foods, drinks and clothing, as well as their dangerous sides, and how to deal with these dangers by using the advice of the best ancient authorities.' Manuals such as the *Tacinium Sanitatis* shared with the Galenic works the premise that all foods had humoral values, i.e. dry, moist, hot or cold, or some combination of these. Food was not neutral, but as part of the material world also possessed the qualities of the humours. Food types might be hot, dry, cold or moist, or a combination of these. Thus, to take a single example from the *Tacinium*, fennel was warm and dry, useful for the eyesight and for keeping down fevers, but it might also be dangerous to women in interfering with menstruation; however, this danger could be neutralized through taking carob seeds to counterbalance its effects.[4]

Diet, therefore, was critical in maintaining the humoral balance. A person suffering from a fever clearly exhibited hot and wet symptoms, and was thus considered to be suffering from a surfeit of sanguine humours. The solution was an intake of cold and dry substances to redress the balance. The humoral theory also lent itself to preventative care. Eating food known to have the property of heat, for example, counteracted a humoral tendency toward cold, or toward an illness producing such an effect. Selecting the appropriate food to eat was a question of balancing different considerations.

Scientific texts on food values also distinguished between the value or benefit of cooked and raw food, recognizing that what might be indigestible or produce negative effects when in a raw state could be beneficial when cooked. Wheat was considered to be the best of the grains, probably for the blood, but barley was suitable for those with a hot constitution. Barley water, which was both moist and cold, helped alleviate chest ailments by treating both heat and thirst. Rice was an example of a food whose value changed with cooking: in its natural inedible state it was thought to constrict the bowels, but when boiled and seasoned it became good for them. Legumes and pulses had mixed benefits: broad beans were considered cold, and if boiled with vinegar were thought to inhibit bowel movement; chickpeas were considered naturally hot, and they were beneficial when boiled, being more nutritious and producing a broth that helped treat kidney stones; while lentils were considered cold and dry, and thus counteracted those with naturally hot temperaments. As we have seen, eating beans undressed with oil or vinegar was part of the Lenten diet in some Byzantine monasteries. Here, a religious taboo may coincide with notions of healthy eating. It may, indeed, be that the Lenten diet evolved from the need to provide balance throughout the year in the ways in which potentially harmful combinations of food were eaten.

One of the earliest sources for our knowledge of the medieval understanding of how diet affected health comes from the book called *The Observation of Foods*, by Anthimus, a member of the court of Theodoric, the Ostrogothic king of Italy in the late fifth century. It may even have been written for the king, who despite his Gothic birth had grown up in Constantinople and was a highly literate Greek speaker. In his preface, Anthimus explains that we should aim for balance in the kinds of food we eat, just as a builder will mix lime and water for cement in the right proportions, in the knowledge that the cement will only work if the quantities of each are right. He goes on to say that for those living in the civilized world, the regulation of diet through variety is essential. It is true, he admits, that there are peoples in the world who can subsist on only one kind of food, but that is because they live in regions where they have had to adapt to their environments or follow lifestyles that demand it. Barbarian peoples can stomach raw meat because they are pastoralists who keep large herds of livestock but grow little food of their own; they therefore live largely on meat and milk, the produce of their herds. On the other hand, Romans, who have the luxury of enjoying different foods and delicacies and different drinks, must regulate their diet if they want to keep their health.

Anthimus' little book is not particularly Galenic in its approach. Although Anthimus accepts uncritically the four humours theory underlying the medicine of his day, his book is more practical than theoretical. It seems rather to combine sound practical observation with an element of folklore. His main concern is to show how foods that might threaten one's health should be cooked or eaten so as to ensure that they are not harmful. Thus, beef should always, according to Anthimus, be casseroled by cooking it slowly in fresh water, then mixed with vinegar, leeks and parsley or fennel, to which honey, pepper, cloves and spikenard are added after longer cooking. Mutton is good either roasted or cooked in gravy, but loin of pork should only be roasted, and never eaten with sauce. Nothing gives more pleasure than bacon, but it should not be roasted because the fat falls into the fire and dries out the meat, so instead it should be boiled and then cooled before eating. Bacon should never be eaten fried either, because it is bad for the health, although bacon fat might be used for cooking when no oil was available. Raw bacon, on the other hand, is very good for the digestion because it cleans out the guts, expels worms and tones up the stomach. It can also be used, apparently, as a poultice for treating wounds. Anthimus also had rules and recommendations about fruit and vegetables: mallow, beets and leeks are healthy all the year round, but cabbages only in winter; mustard greens and turnips are only good when boiled and eaten with bacon and vinegar; parsnips, which have the benefit of promoting urine, should be eaten either boiled or par-boiled, then sautéed; while cucumber seeds are a good remedy for kidney problems.[5]

Fruit could be eaten fresh or dried, but here again the humoral and nutritional effects altered according to the state. Fresh figs and grapes were considered the most nourishing, but dried figs eaten by themselves, being hot and dry, produced blood and gas and could be harmful to those with hot constitutions. Dates, also hot, were nutritional, but could cause digestive trouble, especially bloating of the stomach. Plums came in two kinds: the ripe sweet fruit were less moist and cold, whereas when unripe they could help to move bowels and lower fevers. Apples, which were moist and cold, invigorated the liver and heart. Digestive problems occupied a significant role in the dietary texts. As we have seen, monks like Bernard of Clairvaux and Hilarion, who maintained strict and repetitive diets over a number of years, suffered from poor digestions late in life. Remedies could be found in common monastic food, taken in the right way. Figs, dried and fresh, were good if eaten before the meal as an hors d'oeuvre, but bad for the digestion if eaten as a dessert. Obstructed bowels could be alleviated by drinking the water from the cooking of lentils or cabbage, particularly if flavoured with olive oil. The same was true of the water in which crustaceans had been cooked. Water used to cook fenugreek purged unhealthy humours from the digestion, especially if mixed with a little honey. Beets, sorrel and other herbs, though in some manuals considered to produce bad humours, could be beneficial in purging the bowels in the same way.

Similarly, the manuals recommended eating different kinds of food at different seasons of the year. In January, for example, garlic was recommended for seasoning all foods; rocket, leeks, celery, rue, mint and lovage were also suggested. In February, however, no beets or wild vegetables were to be eaten, whereas throughout

March, sweet flavours were thought advisable, albeit in moderation. Some of this advice is logical in the sense that it corresponds to the kinds of foods naturally in season at a given time of year. Most wild vegetables are not at their best, or indeed edible, in the winter months before the first growth of the spring, or in high summer when seed pods and heads have formed. Above all, the intention was to aim at moderation and balance.

But it is surely no coincidence that the seasonal cycle governing the availability of food also corresponded in some ways to the liturgical cycle observed in monasteries. Although fasts and feasts were scattered throughout the Church's calendar, there were two main periods of fast: Advent and Lent. In the medieval West, Lent in particular was observed by the laity as well as in monasteries. There are, of course, spiritual reasons for the adoption of fasting in these periods: Advent was a period of preparation for the coming of the Messiah at Christmas, while Lent was from the very beginning of the Church's life a time of introspection and penitence in preparation for the commemoration of the Resurrection. The spirituality of Lent demanded a measure of personal and communal austerity, which made giving up meat, wine and other delicacies a natural step for the Church to take. Although the date of Easter can vary by some weeks from year to year, Lent always falls within the period of late winter and early to mid-spring – and it is this period in which fresh meat was in any case likely to have been least available, since livestock were usually slaughtered for eating from late spring to autumn, while the season for game had already ended by the time Lent began. On the other hand, in the Mediterranean lands where the liturgical and dietary customs of the Church first originated, the period of Lent coincides with the time when wild plants and herbs first come into season and are at their best for eating, before the full growth of summer. Lent was thus less of a hardship, even for a strictly observant community.

WILD FOOD

Some of the wild food gathered by hermits and monks is known to us by name, but about much of it we can only speculate. However, we can be sure that both hermits and anchorites living in the wilderness and monks living in communities gathered food in the wild. The early Christian and Orthodox sources are, on the whole, more specific than medieval Western accounts, which tend to speak generically of 'herbs' or 'roots' rather than naming species. But we know that wild-growing onions, leeks and garlic were gathered and eaten, that reeds and melagria (asphodel) were collected by Palestinian hermits for consumption, and that monks in the Judaean desert went out of the coenobium of Euthymius to gather the leaves of the wild chickpea. The *Life of Macarius* also mentions generic herbs that may be thyme or marjoram, but that can certainly be eaten raw as a salad. Naturally, most monks and hermits harvested whatever grew close at hand, which meant that their habitats were chosen with a view to providing enough to live on. Only grazers followed the food.

For would-be hermits of today, there follows a brief digest of wild herbs and vegetables commonly found throughout Europe and the Mediterranean, with suggestions for how they might be cooked or eaten, even by a hermit equipped with only a simple pot.

*   *   *

Alexanders must certainly have been cultivated in medieval monasteries because they can still be found growing wild around the sites of some monastic gardens in England even though the plants are native to the Mediterranean, where they grow in profusion in the wild. In taste, alexanders share similarities with both celery and parsley, and the leaves as well as the stalk are edible. They have a mild aniseed flavour. The stalks can be boiled or sautéed in oil or butter; they are at their best in early spring. A seventeenth-century herbal, Parkinson's *Theatrum botanicum*, suggests making a broth with the root but eating the leaves boiled separately, and recommends eating alexanders as a way of counteracting the effects of too much fish in Lent.

Cleavers (*Galium aparine* or goosegrass), a hedgerow plant related to the woodland herb woodruff, was used in early Welsh medicine for skin problems. The leaves can be made into an infusion and drunk. It was also used to dispel fats from greasy soups and stews. Dioscorides remarked that cleavers were sometimes used in place of a strainer for milk and other liquids. However, they does not seem to have been eaten, except by geese.

Hogweed, sometimes called 'cow parsnip', is a hedgerow plant that presents furled leaves in spring and early summer, when it is at its best. Although most commonly used until recently as pig food, it is not dissimilar to asparagus in flavour. It can be eaten as a salad or steamed and tossed in butter. In Russia, hogweed is dried in the sun until the leaves emit a syrup, which can be used as a sugar substitute; alternatively, it can be left to ferment and used as an alcoholic drink.

Fat hen is also known colloquially, at least in Britain, as 'white goosefoot', 'dungweed' or 'muckweed' because of its prevalence on muck heaps and wasteland; it is also often found at field edges. Fat Hen has been eaten for millennia. Seeds from the plant were found in the stomach of Tollund Man, the prehistoric body preserved in a peat bog in Denmark. It can be eaten raw, particularly if young shoots are cut in spring, or blanched and tossed in oil or butter. Its bluish-green leaves, if allowed to grow to summer maturity, can be used like spinach, though to Patience Gray, the author of *Honey from a Weed*, they taste like broccoli. Fat Hen is known in parts of Italy as 'la saponava', because of its cleansing properties. The American botanist Merritt Fernald reported using the leaves dried, ground and made into bread or muffins.

Sea kale is a cabbage-like plant that grows from the Atlantic to Baltic coasts. Its stalk and flower heads are edible. The flower heads and stalk resemble purple sprouting broccoli and can be cooked in the same way, although they are closer to asparagus in flavour. The leaves are best avoided. Its health-giving properties have been recognized since antiquity, and it was used by sailors to counter scurvy. In the Middle Ages sea kale was cultivated by forcing it under covers so that the young shoots could grow. Like dandelion and other wild but once profusely growing herbs, it was once harvested for sale in inland markets.

Sea beet grows near coastlines. It has thick, tough leaves, so although it can be used as a spinach substitute, it is better cooked than as a salad. It also makes excellent soup or purée.

Marsh samphire, also known as glasswort, grows near coasts or in tidal zones. It is particularly prolific in low-lying coastal mud flats such as around Norfolk or south Wales in Britain, or in the Low Countries. Its side shoots are a little like asparagus in texture, and should be cooked in the same way. It can be picked up to the end of August, but it is not as versatile as some other wild herbs, and is really only good when cooked. However, in Italy, it is also eaten raw with wine vinegar as a salad; in Catalonia, it is pickled in vinegar. **Rock samphire**, which grows in cliffs, is much harder to gather, but equally good for pickling.

Watercress, the aquatic cousin of nasturtium, grows almost everywhere in northern Europe and the Mediterranean. The Greek general Xenophon fed it to his soldiers as a pick-me-up, and it is indeed full of vitamins A and C, and iron. In Ireland, where it grows abundantly, an old tradition associates it with hermits and holy men, surely because it formed an important staple in their diet. Best eaten raw, watercress can also make a delicious soup.

Dandelion is a much overlooked but versatile wild herb indigenous to Europe and Asia. Dandelion can be used to make a drink or as a green vegetable. As late as the nineteenth century, dandelion was sold at markets in England to those without the leisure to gather it themselves. Its root, dried and roasted, can be used as a coffee substitute, like chicory. Infused, dandelion can make a tea with diuretic properties. Its leaves and shoots, which are rich in vitamins A and C, can be sautéed and used like endives. Because they are bitter, they are sometimes – but not by hermits! – cooked in bacon fat. A Greek recipe recommends chopping the leaves, tossing them in olive oil and cooking with pine nuts. In Girona, in Catalonia, pheasant is cooked with dandelions, but, as with bacon, this would not answer for a real hermit. Dandelion heads can also be eaten raw. The milky sap produced by the root was thought for centuries to have a beneficial effect on the liver and kidneys, and it was therefore used to treat bowel disorders – hence its French name 'pis-en-lit'.

Nettles – if the sting can be avoided – make delicious eating in soups or as a green vegetable tossed in butter or lard. Nettle beer is a mild restorative. In the north of England, dock pudding was made with nettles, onions and oatmeal. Nettles grow wild everywhere in Europe and Asia, and the Tibetan monk Milupa supposedly lived exclusively on them – until he turned green. The beneficial properties of nettle, which is a natural histamine, have been known to countless generations of Europeans, and the herb has been associated with the treatment of rheumatism, gout and arthritis. A Romany custom has it that grasping nettles in bare hands, so that they become inflamed from the sting, combats arthritis. Whether or not this works, nettles are certainly rich in vitamins and iron. It is fitting, given their beneficial properties, that nettles always grow near human habitations, even long-ruined ones, because they need a phosphate-rich soil. A rhyme in Harington's translation of a medieval Salernitan text, the *Regimen Sanitatis*, recommends nettles for promoting sleep and preventing nausea.

Wild garlic grows throughout Europe in woodland and shady areas. Before late spring, the leaves can be eaten raw, and work well as a substitute for chives. The leaves tend to become bitter if cooked for too long, but the bulbs can be used as an alternative to cultivated garlic.

Cow parsley is also known as wild chervil or, more picturesquely, Queen Anne's lace. The young leaves are excellent raw as salad, or added to egg dishes. They need to be picked early, however, for when the stem becomes thick and woody, the leaves will be too tough. In Syria, wild chervil was eaten both raw and cooked.

As a garnish, it should be added just before the end of cooking, because the flavour is very delicate and can be spoilt by heat.

Wild fennel is a very versatile plant. Native to the Mediterranean, its value was recognized as early as the ninth century, when the Emperor Charlemagne decreed that it should be cultivated in the south of France. It became firmly established as a kitchen garden plant in the Middle Ages, and its aniseed flavouring was prized. The whole plant can be eaten blanched or steamed and dressed with olive oil and lemon juice, or tossed in flour and deep fried. Wild fennel is different from the sweet Florentine fennel that has a bulbous root. This is a particularly good herb for hermits, since it goes well with fish.

Wild asparagus grows profusely in dry walls near limestone in Italy and the Pyrenees. It has prickly spines, so should be picked with care. The best eating parts are the long shoots, which are the most tender near the top. The top 4–5 inches can be cut off, boiled and served with oil, or fried. In Catalonia, they are added to omelettes and egg dishes. The season for wild asparagus is unfortunately very short, just a few weeks from late March.

Wild hops (*Lupulus humulus*) are native to northern Europe. Although hops are now grown largely for their role in flavouring beer, this use was unknown until the late Middle Ages, at least in England. While it is the flowers that flavour the beer, for eating, the shoots are the valuable part of the plant. They should be boiled or steamed quickly, and make an excellent accompaniment to eggs. They can also be eaten like asparagus, though the flavour is a little more bitter. Patience Gray found that in rural Tuscany, they were interchangeable with wild asparagus. This echoes a piece by Elizabeth David, in which she described a seasonal Venetian risotto made with *bruscandoli* which she identified as wild hops rather than asparagus, but which were evidently similar enough to be confused.[6] Today, hop shoots are characteristic of Belgian cuisine, where they are often cooked with a cream sauce, and in central Italy, where, as Patience Gray found, they are eaten plain or – in Rome – made into a soup. Hops were also used medicinally as a pain-killer or sedative.[7] It was hops, apparently – stuffed into a pillow – that cured the insomnia from which King George III suffered. **Tassel hyacinth,** which is related to the grape hyacinth, grows wild on and near limestone. The bulb, but not the leaves or flowers, are edible. Bulbs should be boiled for almost 20 minutes and the outer skins removed. They are good served cold and dressed with oil.

Angelica is found throughout northern Europe, the Far East and central Asia. It grows wild near abandoned ruins, and thus is especially useful for hermits and monks settling in the ruins of old monasteries. Angelica should be gathered in late winter or early spring, before the flowers emerge from their sheaths. The sheaths are boiled or dipped in beaten egg and fried, or cooked over an open fire. Its seeds can also be made into a tea, and its stalks used as a substitute for celery. It is the flowers and stalks that are used today, largely by the confectionary industry as candied decorations for cakes.

Field poppies are found throughout Europe and Asia, especially invading cultivated ground where legumes grow. Because hermits and monks grew and ate beans as a staple, poppies must have been a very common by-product. In western Turkey and the Balkans, poppies are cooked along with cabbage. They should be blanched, then simmered with garlic and perhaps chilli peppers; they can then be pounded in a mortar and added to a dish of olives and sharp hard cheese. Poppy oil can be used against coughs.

Pignut is a weed that grows on pasture land; it has small white flowers and a rhizome that can grow to the size of a golf ball. The rhizome can be eaten raw, and in this state tastes a little like a hazelnut. It has been praised for its 'crisp substance and clean taste'. Alternatively, the rhizome can be simmered in water and treated like a sweet potato. Some caution may be needed on the part of hermits, however: according to John Pechey's *Compleat Herbal of Physical Plants* (1694), pignuts are aphrodisiacs.

*   *   *

Besides these examples, some flowers are also edible, either as food or as the basis of a drink. The bud of broom, for example, can be used in the same way as a runner bean, which it resembles. In the sixteenth and seventeenth centuries, there was a fashion for pickling the buds. Primrose flowers can be used in salads, as can nasturtium.

The most celebrated wild flower for culinary purposes must surely be the elderflower. Its uses are varied: the flower sprays are used to flavour jellies and sorbets, although hermits are more likely to have them eaten them raw; the heads can also be dipped in a tempura batter and deep fried – a particularly common treatment in Italy; and the berries can be cooked along with other hedgerow fruit to make preserves. Both flowers and berries also make drinks: the flowers can be infused in boiled water which is then reheated to produce a cordial; while elderberry wine can be made from the mashed berries, to which sugar syrup and yeast is added – after several months, an alcoholic drink results.

In some cultures, flower bulbs have been eaten. Rhizomes, such as tulips and dahlias, are the best to try.

SOME MONASTIC HERBS

A Feat of Gardening, an English text written in c.1440 by John Gardener, lists among 'potherbs', or green vegetables grown specifically for cooking, a number of herbs: borage, cress, watercress, groundsel, langdebeef [*langue de boeuf* or *Picris echioides*], tansy, calamint, coriander, dill, dittander [*Lepidium latifolium*], hyssop, lavender, mint, mustard, sage, savory, thyme and wood sorrel. These are listed indiscriminately alongside wild plants such as wild celery and alexanders, and cultivated leafy plants that we would categorize as vegetables, such as lettuce, spinach and fennel. Given what we have already said about the connections between health and diet in ancient and medieval medical understanding, the distinction between growing herbs for medical use or for the pot is not great. Herbs that were regarded as having medicinal properties as

well as providing flavouring were particularly prized.[8]
One of these, very commonly grown in monastic gardens, was
sage, whose botanical name, *Salvia*, is related to the word for
health. Although native to the Mediterranean, it was certainly
being grown in English monasteries by 1213, and perhaps considerably earlier. Many herbs had already moved far from their
native habitats during the Roman period, carried by the armies and
settlers into newly conquered territories. The *pax romana* globalized
Nature. Sage was probably used chiefly as a sedative, though its
leaves were also used to clean teeth. Folkloric wisdom held that it
was best picked at dawn on the eve of the feast of St John (23 June).

Hyssop, likewise, is a southern European plant that was naturalized in northern Europe. It has been found growing wild in the
walls of monastic ruins, which indicates that it must once have
been cultivated in monastic gardens. *Le Menagier of Paris* recommended its use in a hot drink, either as a purgative or to soothe
internal or external inflammations; it was also supposed to be good
for coughs. Hyssop was symbolically important to monks because
of its biblical associations – it was thought to be one of the bitter
herbs that God commanded the Israelites to eat with the Passover
meal in Exodus. **Rue** was similarly used as a purifier, but although
it is mentioned in Frankish monastic sources as early as the ninth
century, it does not seem to have been popular in England until the
end of the Middle Ages.

Camomile, which is not edible except as a tea or tisane, was
primarily used for medicinal purposes – it soothes bites and rashes
– or as a cosmetic preparation. Edward II's wardrobe accounts for
1313 show that it was purchased for his personal use. **Elecampane**
(*Inula helenium or* 'hors helene' in Anglo-Saxon) was primarily a
condiment used for making cakes, but it also features in infirmary
accounts and was probably used for cordials. Mixed with honey
and mallow leaves, it purportedly helped in cases of consumption.
Given its size – it grows to four or five feet and has a large rootstock – it was probably more likely to be found in large monastic
gardens, or collected wild. **Dill,** another native Asian plant, was

primarily grown for medicinal usage. Prized by the Romans, to the extent that it now grows wild in the Mediterranean, it was probably imported to Britain early in the Middle Ages, since the English name of the herb derives from the Old English *dilla* (to lull, soothe), which was its primary use.

Coriander, a herb common to all ancient peoples, was regarded as a stimulant and a digestive, but also appreciated for its bacterial properties. The Persian philosopher al-Razi (ca.865–925, better known as Rhazes) recommended taking the seed with endive for headaches and nose bleeds. Coriander was being grown in monastic gardens in Western Europe by the late Middle Ages, but had been known in the Mediterranean much earlier. Culinary uses included adding the seeds to preserves and jams. **Parsley** has been prized in the Mediterranean since classical times, when it had both a symbolic and decorative function at feasts. Such cultural attachments, however, are often based on knowledge of the beneficial properties of a plant, and parsley is particularly rich in vitamins A and C, calcium and magnesium. It serves as a diuretic, has antiscorbutic properties, and is supposedly good for eye complaints such as conjunctivitis. It was grown everywhere in the Middle Ages, and cultivated in monastic gardens to such an extent that it is listed by John Gardener as representative of a whole category of plants, alongside the *allium* family and worts, rather than as a simple herb. Two herbs related to parsley and also commonly found in monastic gardens were **chervil** and **fennel.** Native to the Near East and Balkans, chervil was used in cooking, especially in egg dishes and soups; it was also valued by infirmarers as an anti-spasmodic and for making skin lotions. Fennel, which has a stronger flavour, was used for stomach conditions and as an aperitif and digestive.

Rosemary later came to be known as 'the water of the queen of Hungary' because Isabella, queen consort of Hungary in the sixteenth century, claimed to have received the recipe for oil of rosemary from a hermit to cure her of the paralysis that had afflicted her. The legend is traceable to a note of the recipe supposedly in the queen's hand in a manuscript now in Vienna. Of course, the herb had a much longer history in ancient Mediterranean culinary and medical practice, but probably appeared only quite late in northern Europe, being first attested in England and Flanders in the 1330s. Besides its digestive properties – it became common as a tisane taken after heavy meal in Provence – rosemary was thought to counteract problems of the brain and humoral coldness. Like sage, it was also used to make tooth powder.

Mustard (mostly *Sinapis alba*, which is native to Europe) was grown both for its leaves, which were appreciated in salads, and for its seeds, a curative condiment thought to have digestive properties. The Romans are known to have prepared a paste from the crushed seeds as early as the first century AD, and the Byzantines used mustard in a vinaigrette. In the Middle Ages, growers around Dijon developed the first mustard industry by forming the dried crushed seeds into tablets. *Le Viandier* has a recipe for a 'soupe de moustarde' made from a wine-based bouillon, into which one fried eggs, then added mustard.

Mint, greatly prized in Europe, had been known in the Near East since ancient times as a digestive acting against acid in the stomach and to help clear the bowels. Mint oil and mint tea can be used as a tonic and stimulant. Different varieties of mint appear in very many medieval recipes, but the leaves were also used to ward off fleas. One variety, apple mint, had the nickname 'monks' herb', which indicates its primary use by monastic infirmarers. **Cumin,** which we associate primarily with Eastern and Middle Eastern cooking, was very widely grown in medieval Western Europe, and features as one of the commonest items used as in-kind payments of rent, which means that it must have been grown by the relatively poor in small gardens as well as in monastic gardens. The seeds were crushed and used in a paste to make cosmetics for the skin.

These are just a few of the herbs attested in monastic herbals, or known from other sources to have been cultivated in herb and infirmary gardens. Not all were edible, and since this is a book on food and eating, I have concentrated on those that featured in the pot as well as in the pharmacist's bottle. Infirmarers grew many plants for medicinal use only. The 'Bury herbal', from the abbey of Bury St Edmunds, for example, lists 141 plants grown in the monastery garden, including ivy, henbane, yarrow – also known as bloodwort from its role in staunching bleeding wounds – and cannabis. The leaves of henbane, crushed, could be used as a sedative against pain or emotional distress, but in the wrong quantity, as a poison – as used by the notorious Dr Crippen to murder his wife in 1910. Ivy goes well with monastic ruins – Tintern, as described by Wordsworth, for example – but although it had a powerful symbolic presence, it may also have been grown to answer a long-standing belief in its prophylactic properties. Geoffrey Grigson records the Shropshire tradition of drinking from a cup made of ivy wood to prevent whooping cough.

The cultivation of herbs by monasteries, whether for eating, medicinal uses or both, raises bigger questions about monastic gardening. What place did gardens play in the economy of a typical monastery? What else, apart from herbs, did monks grow in the gardens, and how did they use gardens, fields, rivers and ponds to create the self-sufficient and enclosed communities that St Benedict had envisaged? The next chapter will explore the sources of food in monasteries, from field to table.

Chapter Five

From field to table – the medieval monastic experience

FOOD GROWING

Early monasticism, both solitary and communal, went hand-in-hand with growing food. Pachomius' *Rule* mentions both an orchard for cultivating fruit and palm trees, and a vegetable garden. In the *Sayings of the Fathers*, Gelasius' monastery at Nicopolis was left a plot of land as a bequest from a solitary monk – presumably the plot he had himself tended to grow his own food, and which included a small olive grove. Even Anthony asked for a hoe, an axe and some grain so that he could provide for himself through cultivation. Monks cultivated fresh vegetables even in apparently arid regions. The ability to grow food even in the least welcoming conditions is attested in the story told by the fifth-century author Sulpicius Severus about a monk in Egypt. Despite living in the desert, he grows his own vegetables with the help of a well and an ox. The ox turns the wheel attached to the handle of the well to draw up the water, which keeps a patch of sand moist for growing herbs. As Sulpicius observes, this is remarkable because it goes against Nature, and thus represents the victory of the monk over the desert. Equally surprising was the monk's ability to cook for his visitors without needing to make a fire, for the heat of the sun boiled water by itself. This last detail suggests that Sulpicius, knowingly or otherwise, was passing on a 'myth of the desert' to readers in the West who were avid for stories about monasticism in the exotic Egyptian climate. In fact, we have ample evidence that Egyptian monks cooked food. Sulpicius' Egyptian, however, is an archetype of the self-sufficient hermit who need not rely on the outside world in order to live.[1]

The larger the community, however, the more complex its domestic economy becomes. Monasteries were intended to be self-sufficient institutions in practical affairs as well as spiritual; indeed, they had to be so in order to retain the least possible dependence on society. This effectively meant that monasteries had to be working farms, with agricultural land to produce food and a labour force to work the land. Although almost all monastic founders and legislators regarded some manual labour as spiritually necessary, it was probably not possible for monasteries, once they reached a certain size, to rely entirely on its own monks for such work. For one thing, the expertise required in both the farming and the production of food was probably beyond most monks. This does not mean that monks did none of this work. The twelfth-century Cypriot hermit Neophytos, who had begun his religious career as a monk at the monastery of Koutsovendis, recalled being sent out to work dressing the vines. But this may have been because he was a village boy who was not yet literate; once he had acquired some education in the monastery, he was moved to other duties.

There may thus have been a distinction between what was expected of monks in the way of manual labour depending on their suitability, or lack of it, for more refined work. Cluny, which farmed out most of its lands indirectly to tenants, preserved the custom of 'ritualized' labour in the kitchen garden well into the twelfth century. Between Pentecost and November, as long as it was not a feast day, the monks might be required to weed the rows of beans and peas. The ritual quality of the occasion was emphasized by the psalm-singing that preceded it, and the special drink of wine flavoured with honey and absinthe that followed. This light work, no doubt agreeable enough on a pleasant day, fulfilled the *Rule's* demand for manual labour while not taking up too much of the monks' time.

This provides another reason why relatively little of the food growing and food production was done by monks: notoriously at

Cluny and its dependents, but probably also at many other large and well-endowed monasteries, the liturgy had grown to the point where it was simply impossible to spare sufficient time for the monks to engage in regular work. In 1063, the reformer Peter Damian observed – doubtless with some exaggeration – that there was scarcely half an hour to spare between the end of one office and the next. All this meant that in large monasteries, in both the East and West, the monastic community itself became increasingly distanced from the business of providing its own food.

By the twelfth century, large monasteries organized food production through 'granges' – farms at some distance from the abbey itself. Cluny organized its granges so that each one was responsible for providing the staples of bread, beans and fatty foods for the community. The proportions were adjusted to take into account crop diversity and agrarian conditions; thus, the grange at Mazille grew more oats than corn, so it provided the bulk of the feed for the abbey's horses, whereas Jully and St Hippolyte, which were in grape-growing districts, provided the wine.

Food production was one of the things about monasticism that the reformers of the eleventh and twelfth centuries most wanted to change. The Cistercians were particularly concerned about manual labour. The result was that they insisted on direct farming of their lands, rather than leasing out their landed property to tenant farmers. It did not mean, however, that the monks themselves did all, or even much, of the actual farming. Although early Cistercians were mocked for 'smelling of the fields', as one Cluniac put it, they were probably no more able to provide food directly from their own hands than any of the monasteries whose failings they criticized. Instead the Cistercians used lay brothers, known as 'conversi', to do much of the farming for them. Typically the work was done at granges, which were supposed to be no more than a day's journey from the monastery.

The Cistercians made their mark by settling in regions only newly colonized for farming, such as north Yorkshire, Scotland and Wales, and the central European and Baltic lands that were only just, in the twelfth century, becoming part of Christian Europe. However, in areas such as southern France and Italy that were part of the 'heartland' of Europe, many Cistercian monasteries were not new foundations at all but existing reform houses that joined the Cistercian congregation. In what we might call 'frontier regions', Cistercian husbandry tended to be dominated by large-scale and far-flung enterprises – sheep farming in Wales and northern England, for example. In contrast, Cistercian granges in the Camargue grew grain such as rice.

The Cistercians were not the only monastic Order to use lay brothers in their economy, but they extended their use further than any other. Because the lay brothers were technically members of the monastic community, with their own regulations and constitutions and required to live in separate quarters in the monastery when they were not actually serving at a grange, their manual labour counted on behalf of the whole community. This meant that the full monks ('choir monks', as they were known) did not have to perform any manual labour, because the work done by the lay brothers counted for the community as a whole.

A description of one of the early Cistercian monasteries, Clairvaux in Champagne, survives from the early twelfth century. The monastery had only been in existence since 1115, when it was founded by the dynamic St Bernard. The monastery had vegetable and herb gardens for the monks' own eating needs, as well as an orchard, vineyard and fish pond. The orchard was planted next to the infirmary, so that convalescent monks could sit on the grass under the trees, taking the air while sheltered from the sun. Beyond the orchard lay the garden, divided by a network of little streams in which fish swam. The streams, of course, irrigated the garden as well as providing a habitat for the fish. They had been diverted from a tributary of the river Aube, beside which the monastery had been established. The presence of the stream meant that a watermill could be built to mill the grain grown in the abbey's fields. On one side of the river stood the lay-brothers' buildings, including a barn storing the ploughs and yokes, and a meadow had been flooded to create a sizable fish pond. Where once farm labourers sweated as they scythed the meadow, says the anonymous author of this piece in a rather heavy-handed figure of speech, now a monk glides in a wooden horse over the water with a pole to speed his progress in place of spurs. Fishing was done with nets from the punt. Although the author does not give any details about the food grown in the gardens themselves, the intention of the account is clearly to demonstrate that most of the immediate needs of a strict Benedictine diet could be met from the monastery's own local environment and from the efforts of the monks and lay brothers.

Gerald of Wales was certainly impressed by the energies of Cistercians in turning uncultivated land into productive arable and pasture. In a year, he exclaimed, they could turn a barren retreat in an overgrown forest into a productive monastic estate. However, give the Cluniacs productive land and fine buildings, and they will ruin it and reduce it to poverty – they would rather let their manors and farms collapse and the poor starve at their gates than forego a single of the courses to which they claim to be entitled at dinner.[2]

MONASTIC GARDENS AND ORCHARDS

Only a short distance from the River Jordan and a few miles south-east of the ancient town of Jericho lies the monastery of St Gerasimus. The monastery church was built over the cave in which the Holy Family supposedly hid from Herod on their flight from Bethlehem to Egypt. The landscape is flat and sandy. Near the northern tip of the Dead Sea, the climate here is moderate in winter but extremely hot in summer. St Gerasimus provides one of the best examples of cultivation in the semi-desert. Approaching the monastery from the road, one is confronted with the massive walls behind which the dome of the church shelters. A little closer and the monastery begins to look like an oasis: trees and vines form an arbour outside the gate, while inside, the courtyard is delightfully planted with trees and shrubs. Birds fill the place with their song, and chickens and cockerels wander about nonchalantly. But it is only when one walks around the back of the compound that the real surprise of St Gerasimus becomes evident. The monastery still has its own functioning garden and orchard, as well as a large ornamental garden. When I visited one February, rows of lettuces, cabbages, chard and spinach were growing in the mild winter climate. In the orchard, there were figs, olives, date palms and banana trees; turkeys strutted among them, and in a separate paddock there were goats and sheep. On the same day, there was still snow on the ground in Jerusalem, high in the Judaean hills, while only about 17 miles to the west the monks of St Gerasimus sat in their balmy and verdant courtyard.

The monks of St Gerasimus have modern irrigation techniques to help them make the desert bloom. Even so, they are following a venerable tradition in growing food even in the most inhospitable conditions. The Great Laura of Sabas in the Kidron Valley looks today as though nothing except cacti and a few desert weeds could ever grow there, but archaeological and literary evidence both indicate that fresh fruit and vegetables were grown in the wadi. Cisterns were dug to collect water, not only from rainfall on the monastery site, but also from conduits some way off from the wadi. The passage of water throughout the whole site indicates the need to provide water for the complex of cells that made up the laura of St Sabas in its early days. The sixth-century monk of the laura, Cyril of Scythopolis, asserted that no trees could grow in the laura. In the wadi bed, where there was a deep layer of soil, monks tried to plant fig trees, but even with assiduous watering throughout the winter they found it almost impossible. In Cyril's *Life of John the Hesychast,* a fig tree not only takes root by John's cell but even bears three figs, which is regarded as miraculous by the monks who had tried and failed to grow them in the wadi bed. North of the laura, however, a smaller monastery, also built by St Sabas, succeeded in growing a fruit orchard. Archaeologists found evidence of agricultural terraces and cisterns for collecting water dating from the early Byzantine period. An experimental planting of olive trees on the site in the 1980s to test conditions proved successful. Perhaps the soil bed is deeper here, or perhaps irrigation was better because of the proximity of this monastery to another wadi branching off the Kidron at this point. Another monastic founder, Cyriacus, succeeded in growing vegetables at a site about 12 miles south of St Sabas, so it cannot have been impossible for the monks of the laura to have tended their own little plots next to their cells, and the cisterns would have made watering possible all year round.

Pilgrims to the monastery of St Katherine in Sinai in the thirteenth and fourteenth centuries described an orchard growing apples, vines, figs, dates and nuts. Medieval Western monasteries, of course, found it much easier to grow fruit and vegetables. Gardens and gardening were a vital part of the economy of Western Europe by the later Middle Ages. English documentary records and archaeological evidence indicate that besides the well-managed gardens of great aristocratic households and monasteries, even peasant houses in many villages had gardens for growing vegetables. The allotment culture evidently has a long and distinguished history.

Because gardens were so common a feature of medieval monastic life, garden produce does not always appear in the records, except when payments are recorded for garden labour or when surplus produce was sold. A window has been left open, however, to the gardens at Norwich Cathedral Priory, by the survival of the accounts of the gardener. At Norwich, the gardener was one of the obedientaries (monks appointed to an official responsibility within the monastery). He was subordinate to the cellarer, who had overall responsibility for the food supplies, and, probably because the gardens had a relatively small financial turnover, he was lowest in status of all the obedientaries. The annual income from the garden varied between £2 and £17 annually, but it never amounted to more than 0.5 per cent of the total income of Norwich Priory. The gardener had charge of several garden plots dotted around the monastic complex, wedged between the larder, cookhouse, pounding-mill, malt house, wheat granary and slaughterhouse in the outer courtyard. In addition, he was responsible for the use of meadows, a cherry orchard, a pear and apple orchard and several stands of trees.[3]

The plants grown at Norwich were mostly for food, though there were also some cash crops, such as madder, teasels and hemp. We can reconstruct what must have been grown from the receipts recorded for the sale of surplus vegetables and plants. In the fourteenth and fifteenth centuries, these comprised beans, peas, garlic, apples, pears, filberts and porrets. The gardener also sold wax (from beehives), madder, eggs, teasels and wood blown down in storms. The list of plants sold corresponds fairly closely with what we know of other English monastic gardens. Huge quantities of garlic seem to dominate. At Glastonbury Abbey, for example, garlic was grown in sufficient quantities to allow for three cloves per monk per day, whereas the orchard could only provide a single apple a week for each monk. Some of this was probably grown for medicinal purposes, but even so, quite a lot must have been used for cooking. The notion that garlic is a relatively recent Mediterranean import into northern European cuisine is, apparently, a myth.

In the nature of garden produce, of course, such calculations are bound to be artificial because the produce is seasonal; for example, there might have been a glut of apples in autumn and winter, but none in spring or summer. Monastery gardens, like those of great aristocratic estates, probably covered at least a couple of acres – for example, the smaller Somerset abbey of Meare had a garden and orchard of about two and a half acres combined. However, others were at least five acres or more, such as the garden at Ely Cathedral Priory which covered six acres. And at Peterborough, the abbot's garden – presumably growing food for the abbot's household, but also including the 'New Herber', a pleasure garden planted in 1302 – covered six acres, and the cellarer had his own kitchen garden which must have been about the same size. Some were enormous – Bury St Edmunds boasted a total of 40 acres, although this must have included meadow and pasture as well.

Before about 1300, the main vegetables grown in northern European gardens were onions (including shallots and spring onions), leeks, colewort (a green-leafed vegetable similar to spinach or chard), peas, beans and parsley. The treatise *A Feat of Gardening*, from about 1440, categorizes three kinds of vegetable: onions, leeks and garlic; colewort (kale) and other worts; and parsley. The main culinary function of these plants was to flavour and enrich pottage, or soup, which was the staple dish of all households, secular as well as monastic. Root vegetables that we might consider essential for soups, particularly the carrot, do not seem to have been introduced into northern Europe before the fourteenth century, and were not common in England until the fifteenth; at any rate, they are scarcely mentioned by *A Feat of Gardening*, nor do they appear in cookery books. Carrots were known in the Middle East, however, particularly in Arabic cooking, from at least the tenth century, and may have been used more commonly in Byzantine monastic kitchens, though probably as a salad rather than in soups. At this time, there were two main varieties of carrot: one purple-red and the other white – orange carrots did not appear before the

Pottage

This recipe is for a thin vegetable-based soup rather than one thickened with grains. A variety of greens can be used. Place a large onion, two or three leeks, half a cabbage and the same number of turnips into a pot with water; bring to the boil. Add salt and pepper and a bay leaf, simmer and continue cooking until the mixture has reduced to produce a vegetable stock. Discard the vegetables. Collect a good handful of mixed greens such as kale, mustard greens, spinach, chard or Chinese leaf, and a smaller handful of parsley. Shred the leaves and add them to the stock; bring to the boil and cook for 4 minutes. If a thicker soup is desired, a small handful of porridge oats can be added with the greens, or alternatively suet dumplings – but be sure to use vegetable suet!

seventeenth century. Monastery gardens, like aristocratic gardens, also seem to have sold produce, acting both as market gardens for neighbourhoods where not enough fresh produce would otherwise have been available, and as trade nurseries selling seed.

Besides orchards, woods and forests were vital resources both for hermits and monastic communities. They were obvious resorts for the hermit who needed to sustain him- or herself in the wild, but the nuts, berries and wild herbs and vegetables that were so abundant between spring and autumn were also valuable for monastic communities. Reform monasteries in the eleventh and twelfth centuries had an ambivalent attitude to woodland. In the *First Life* of Bernard of Clairvaux, as in Walter Daniel's *Life of Aelred of Rievaulx*, the imagery of monks taming the wildest parts of nature is explicit. Thick forests that had once been the lairs of wild beasts became rich with well-watered gardens through the industry of the monks. However, not all woodland was tamed, for woods left alone or managed carefully provided fuel in the form of thick underbrush, trees for building materials, and of course honey from bees. Where there was honey, there was also beeswax for candles. This is why the charters of so many Western monasteries record in detail the rights of monks to harvest woodland resources. Monks also, of course, kept bees in hives in monasteries – sometimes in secret, as in the example of the two monks of Dunstable Priory who in 1443 were found to have kept the honey for themselves rather than sharing it with the community.

Unlike Benedictine and Orthodox monasteries, most Carthusians did not have extended communal gardens. Instead, each monk had his own small plot behind his cell in which he could grow whatever he pleased. At Mount Grace Priory in North Yorkshire, these individual gardens can still clearly be seen in outline. In some Carthusian monasteries, such as Hinton in Somerset, the gardens had paved walks, evidently for the monks to take exercise. The gardens here were about 73 square feet. At Mount Grace, a wooden overhang ran along the cloister wall of all the gardens for shelter against the Yorkshire rain. Excavations at Mount Grace have shown that monks were imaginative in their designs for their gardens. One had a tiled-roofed overhang all the way around and an outside toilet; another had a tank that may have served as a decorative pond. We know from the *Life of St Hugh of Lincoln* that, in his days as a Carthusian monk at La Chartruese, Hugh used to tame birds and squirrels in his garden – until the prior forbad this as an interference with a monk's solitude.

THE CELLARER

The task of ensuring the transition from growing to eating in a monastery fell to the cellarer. He was the head of the commissariat in the typical Benedictine monastery. As with all such offices, the cellarer was a monk who had been appointed specially to the role by the abbot. It was his job to ensure that a regular supply of food was available to the kitchen. He was also responsible for the cooking and eating utensils for cellar, kitchen and refectory. At Cluny the job was subdivided, with a chamberlain taking on responsibility for the storage of all food except bread, wine and vegetables, which were part of the cellarer's empire. The cellarer had to keep a record of all livestock in the farms and granges, and the fish ponds, dairies and pigsties also came under his supervision. He had four subordinates: the granary-keeper, who had charge of the bakery; the vineyard-keeper; the gardener, who was responsible for providing vegetables for the refectory from the kitchen gardens; and the keeper of the fish ponds.

The cellarer also checked the daily dietary needs of the monks in the infirmary and supplied food as required for the infirmary kitchen. It was his task to ensure that the feasts and fasts were observed correctly in the refectory, and to keep the kitchens supplied in advance with the appropriate food for each. Benedict had insisted that the *Rule* should be read and expounded in instalments in chapter throughout the year, to remind monks of their obligations. The custom at Cluny, also borrowed by monasteries such as Christ Church Canterbury, was that on the day when the cellarer's role was read and explained, he was to provide a feast for the whole community in the refectory. The Chronicle of Abingdon Abbey in Oxfordshire lists not only the duties, but even the ideal character of the cellarer. He should be humble, kind and merciful, capable of observing self-discipline himself, but indulgent toward others. So complex were his duties, that by the late twelfth century the cellarer was absolved of all other duties, except celebration of Mass and attendance at the daily chapter.

The job of the cellarer in a large monastery was difficult enough; with an obstructive abbot, it could be impossible. This is very clear from Jocelyn of Brakelond's account of Bury St Edmunds in the late twelfth century. The whole monastery seems to have been insolvent, and in order to keep the food supplies coming in, the cellarer borrowed money on his own account. When the abbot – Samson's predecessor – found that the debt had reached £60, he sacked the cellarer from his office. The cellarer of Bury, however, had what sounds like a legitimate grievance. He complained that for the past three years he had been expected to give hospitality to the monastery's guests out of his income, even though guests who arrived when the abbot was in the monastery were supposed to be entertained at the abbot's table. The justice of this complaint was seen when only a few days later the new cellarer found three knights and their squires in the guest house waiting to be fed. He went straight to the abbot with the keys to the cellars and offered to resign unless the abbot agreed to receive and entertain the guests.[4]

This was a point of domestic economy on which feelings ran high, and for good reason. In most monasteries, the abbot's household was run on separate lines from that of the rest of the monastery, and often had separate income streams in the form of property and endowments. An abbot who did not fulfil his responsibilities by entertaining guests was forcing the community into expenditure that it might not be able to afford. On the other hand, Abbot Samson, the hero of Jocelyn's chronicle, was determined to keep up the traditional custom of entertaining guests as long as he was in the abbey. According to this custom, if the abbot was away, the cellarer should entertain up to thirteen guests with horses at the abbey's expense; more than that, and they were to be entertained by the abbot's servants. The only exception was that guests who were themselves monks had to eat in the refectory with the community. This was a fundamental matter of principle, for in all early monastic rules, both Eastern and Western, care was taken not to give monks any licence to stray from the dietary norms of the rule when they were outside their monastery on business.

Not all the problems were on one side, of course. Abbot Samson was to find that one reason for the debts incurred by the former cellarer at Bury was that he and the prior were holding private parties in the prior's quarters, and that the guest-master, who had responsibility for the accommodation of guests, was recklessly extravagant. When he investigated, Samson found that all three blamed each other. When he asked the rest of the community, one monk observed that, judging by the food served in the refectory, the trouble certainly couldn't be extravagance in feeding the monks. In the end, Abbot Samson dismissed the cellarer and took over the office himself, which must have greatly added to his workload, but seems to have helped in restoring the community's fortunes.

THE REFECTORY

Conduct in the refectory was strictly controlled, at least in theory. Benedict's *Rule* stipulated that each monastery must have a refectory where monks should eat in common. In the Byzantine cenobitic reform of the eleventh and twelfth centuries, this was also one of the standard specifications for a new monastery. Because Orthodox monks lived in cells, founders were careful to ensure that no eating was done in private, and that monks could not take food into their cells. Violating this rule would undermine the principle of equality within the community, since it was obviously impossible to ensure that all monks were eating the same food in the same amounts unless the food was served and eaten in community. In Western medieval monasteries, where monks did not have their own cells, this was less of a problem. As we shall see, the question of whether eating could be done *only* in the refectory or also elsewhere became a big issue. Even after the loophole in the *Rule* opened the way for a greater variety of foods to be eaten, the refectory seems to have been respected as a place where the *Rule* should, as far as possible, be observed.

The best place to observe correct conduct in the refectory is in the constitutional decrees passed by the Cistercians, which were designed to ensure that Benedict's *Rule* was followed to the letter. In the earliest set of decrees, passed in 1134, no speaking was allowed in the refectory. Instead monks were supposed to use sign language to make their needs known. Only if a monk was not fluent in sign language and could not make himself understood was he allowed to utter a single word, such as 'bread' or 'water'. The

5.   Refectory pulpit. Bellepais Abbey, northern Cyprus

punishment for violating this rule was to be deprived of wine, or of the cooked dishes for that meal. During dinner, the monks listened to a reading by one of the monks. This might be scriptural, or taken from a commentary or piece of pastoral theology, or even the *Rule* itself. The survival of this custom into the later Middle Ages is attested by the building of special pulpits or balconies for readers in some monasteries. After dinner, the reader and the monks who had done the serving, took their turns at the table.

DRINKING

> *They would not stick*
> *to heal the sick*
> *in body and in soul,*
> *they had such wit they could do it*
> *by drinking of a bowl.*
>
> Robert Crowley (1551),
> Philargyrie of Great Britain, II, pp. 575–80

Gerald of Wales, writing in the late twelfth century, was scandalized to find that the monks of Canterbury regularly drank claret, mulberry wine, mead and other strong liquors. So great was the variety of drinks they were served that there was no room at their tables for ale, even though Kent produced the best in England. The traditional drink for monks and hermits from the earliest days was, of course, water. But both Benedict and his Eastern counterparts were accustomed to wine as the normal drink with a meal, and this found its way on to standard monastic menus. In fact, in areas where vineyards could be planted, it was probably easier to supply quantities of wine than fresh supplies of drinking water. In Mediterranean monasteries throughout the Middle Ages, wine thus remained the standard – and safest – drink except among the very abstemious. Throughout Europe and the Mediterranean, cholera and intestinal infections caught from drinking polluted water were significant causes of premature death in society as a whole, and this applied to the rich as well as the poor, since they must have drunk water from the same rivers. Water from wells was safer, of course, but digging and facing a decent well might be a considerable expense. There is evidence that, in Italy at least, Roman aqueducts continued to be used until well into the Middle Ages, and public water management was a feature of some towns.

The *Rule of Pachomius*, dating from the fourth century, demands that the monks' wine should be mixed with water, but does not give the proportions. Early monastic literature offers conflicting advice on wine drinking. In one story in the Syrian *Paradise of the Fathers*, a monk who ostentatiously refused to drink wine escaped to the roof of his monastery in order to avoid being given a cup of it, but got the just desserts of his pride when the roof gave way under him. Abba Poemen, on the other hand, is recorded in the *Sayings of the Fathers* as ruling that 'the nature of wine is not such as to make it useful to dwellers in monasteries'. Theodore the Studite, whose early ninth-century *Rule* for his newly founded monastery in Constantinople was to prove highly influential in the Byzantine world, recommended a limit of one or two cups daily for monks, except when used as a restorative for the sick or weak, or on feast days.[5]

Some medieval Western reformers used abstinence from wine as a proof of the seriousness of their ascetic intentions. Bernard of Blois, a reformer who lived in a series of monastic communities near Antioch in the early twelfth century, made refusal of wine a point of principle for those monks who followed his rebellion against a prior whom he regarded as too lax in his ways.

Vineyards were planted in England in the Middle Ages. Some of those planted by the Romans were evidently still productive in the Anglo-Saxon period, since a law of Alfred the Great refers to the compensation to be paid by someone damaging vineyards. Alfred's great-grandson Edwy gave a vineyard to Glastonbury Abbey in the mid-tenth century. The Norman Conquest, however, brought new life to viticulture in England, largely because many Norman, French and Italian abbots who were appointed to head English abbeys brought with them both vine plants and the techniques of growing them. At Malmesbury in Wiltshire, a Greek monk, Constantine, planted a vine on the south-facing slope of Hampton Hill in 1084; it was still producing wine two hundred years later. A chronicler of Evesham Abbey celebrated the planting of a vine as one of the major achievements of the new Norman Abbot Walter in the reign of William the Conqueror. Although most viticulture in England took place in the fertile valleys of Gloucestershire, Worcestershire and Herefordshire, monasteries in East Anglia, particularly Ely, Ramsey and Thorney, also grew vines. The abbot of Ramsey, Oswald, had originally come from the famous Cluniac abbey of Fleury-sur-Loire, and had obviously brought his viticultural know-how with him from that famous wine-growing region. One of the problems associated with wine was storage. However, this problem was solved radically, and scandalously, by the abbey of Noyon-sur-Andelle in Normandy: on the visitation of Norman religious houses conducted by Archbishop Eudes of Rouen between 1248 and 1269, Noyon was found to have converted its chapter-house – the building at the heart of daily community life – to usage as a wine cellar.

Ale was the usual drink for monks, as for most laypeople, in northern Europe. It was usually made from malted barley or wheat, depending on which cereal crop grew locally. In the Yorkshire Dales, even oats were sometimes used to make ale. For taste, brewers added whatever local herbs they chose. Hops did not make an appearance, at least in England, until the later Middle Ages. Until then, the malt in ale was flavoured with a variety of herbs and wild plants, including ivy, bog myrtle and yarrow. Once it was discovered that hop flowers had a preservative quality and that ale made with hops kept longer than without, their future was assured. This discovery, in fact, spelled the end for home-brewed ale. Because ale went off quickly, most monasteries, like most major secular households, had their own brewhouse to ensure a regular fresh supply. This meant considerable outlay in terms of space, for brewing on the scale required to supply a large community required huge vats and leads. On the other hand, buying in ale, besides being more expensive, was logistically impractical. Since it did not keep for long periods, it would have had to be imported in large volumes very regularly. The first duke of Buckingham's household in the early fifteenth century consumed 30,000–40,000 gallons of ale every year, which, it has been calculated, would have filled 300 wagons. However, once hops were used regularly, ale-brewing could be carried out on an industrial scale away from where it was to be drunk.

The 'failure of the beer' – meaning the malt harvest – was from time to time recorded lugubriously by the Dunstable chronicler. In 1262 and 1274, wine had to be bought in to replace the beer that was not available, which the chronicler seems to have regarded as a less pleasing alternative. This may mean that English tastes were already favouring beer over wine. In Mediterranean regions, however, beer was regarded as something of an aberration. A health handbook written for the countess of Provence in 1256 by Aldobrandino of Siena advised that beer was bad for the head and the stomach, it gave the drinker bad breath, and filled the

Figure 6   Oven and malt brewery. White Castle, Monmouthshire

brain with bad fumes – although it could have a medicinal use in promoting urine. If one had to drink it, beer made from rye was preferable to wheat or barley beer.

The liking of the English, whether monks or others, for beer was also well known and remarked on in the Middle Ages. Pope Innocent III used beer-drinking to make a joke at the expense of the chronicler of Evesham Abbey, who was in Rome in 1206 to plead a legal case on behalf of his abbey against the bishop of Worcester. After he had made what was regarded as a rather dubious point in canon law, the pope asked where he had learned such an interpretation of the law. In the cathedral schools of England, said the monk. 'Well, you and your teachers must have had too much of your English beer when you learned that!' the pope replied crushingly.[6]

A special Lenten drink was stipulated in some Byzantine typika. This was made from cumin seeds steeped in hot water, or, in the case of the ninth-century monastery of Theodore the Studite, from pepper, caraway seeds and anise in water. It was thought to aid digestion, but was apparently so foul that one typikon has an appendix recording that since it had the effect of making healthy monks sick, it should henceforth be removed from the menu.[7]

USES AND ABUSES OF THE *RULE*: BENEDICTINE EATING IN THE LATER MIDDLE AGES

By the time of the monastic reform in the eleventh and twelfth centuries, many monasteries were finding it difficult to maintain the *Rule of Benedict* when it came to diet. Indeed, the rhetoric of reformers such as the Cistercians, and the admiration for the practices of the austere Carthusians, only makes sense if we accept that most monasteries probably did not stick closely to regulations about food. The most blatant example probably concerns the eating of meat. Benedict himself may have allowed that two-footed animals did not count as meat, which obviously gave monasteries scope for serving fowl; in any case, by the twelfth century, monastic commentaries on the *Rule* seem to have taken the eating of chicken and other fowl for granted.

Further relaxations to the *Rule* developed over time. A twelfth-century monk of Bury St Edmunds, Jocelyn of Brakelond, wrote an illuminating account of the abbey's history and domestic economy during the abbacy of Samson (c.1180s–1211). It is apparent from Jocelyn that definitions of what constituted 'meat' were far from simple. Benedict had prohibited eating the flesh of four-footed animals. But what about parts of the animal that could not literally be defined as 'flesh', or the muscle tissue that most of us probably imagine when we think of meat? Was offal, for example – or processed meat such as sausages, or haggis, or 'umbles' (sheep entrails cooked with ale and bread) – really 'meat' in the same way as a fresh cut off the joint? Gerald of Wales, a contemporary of Jocelyn, complained that some monasteries even served bacon on the grounds that it was not to be considered proper meat. A distinction was thus observed between 'meat' as such and dishes made with meat treated or prepared with other foods, such as pies, rissoles and so on – perhaps even pilaffs where rice was available. Some meats, such as pork, lent themselves particularly to such distinctions. Sausages, blood pudding and liver sausage, all of which had to be made in the pig-slaughtering season of winter (December being the traditional month), were particularly plentiful in the weeks before and after Christmas. These foods tended to be made from the part of the animal left over after the best cuts had been taken off to be preserved, and so had to be eaten quite quickly. They certainly had to be finished off before Lent, when meat products disappeared altogether from the diet.

Monasteries following the *Rule of Benedict* were, technically, autonomous institutions that could develop their own customs and ways of observing the *Rule*. By 1215, however, the papacy was concerned about the lack of quality control over monastic practices: there was huge variety in the ways in which monasteries all over Europe observed the *Rule*, and the most fundamental concern as to who had authority to check on what happened inside monasteries. In theory, in both the Catholic West and the Orthodox East, monasteries were subject to the authority of the local bishop. However, over time, many monasteries developed claims to freedom from such jurisdiction, with the result that by the thirteenth century there seemed to be little or no uniformity to the constitutional position of monasteries that were not already part of an order such as the Cistercians or Carthusians. This was one of the issues of internal governance in the Church that Pope Innocent III addressed in his Fourth Lateran Council in 1215. From that date on, all monasteries were, in theory, subject to oversight in the form of regular 'visitations' by bishops and annual general meetings of all abbots at which proper observance of the *Rule* could be checked. It is debatable how far these annual meetings, known as 'chapters', were able to enforce correct observance, but at least they identified breaches and sought ways to make questionable practices conform to a centrally agreed code of conduct. In this way, a number of loopholes that had emerged could be rationalized into a system.

One such loophole that concerned food was the definition of the refectory. This was important because the *Rule of Benedict* only specified what was to be eaten within the refectory. This was presumably not because Benedict himself wished to leave open a possible loophole for dubious eating habits, but rather because, having stipulated in the *Rule* that each monastery should have a common eating place for the monks, he assumed that this was where all the monks would as a matter of course eat. By the thirteenth century, and perhaps earlier, monks had found a way around this: only the food eaten in the refectory was in theory governed by the dietary prescriptions in the *Rule*. Anything might be consumed, hypothetically, in other parts of the monastery. A papal concession for the priory of St Augustine's, Canterbury allowed the monks to eat meat in the hall and in the abbot's own rooms.[8] At many monasteries, a special supplementary room, known as the 'misericord' (literally 'place of mercy') was built apart from the refectory for this purpose. This was not necessarily seen as a loophole. One of the earliest set of post-Lateran monastic statutes from England, dating from 1219, recommends that monasteries provide a room off the cloister where monks can take recreation and eat whatever and whenever they want – even meat.

By the late Middle Ages, the misericord was an accepted part of the monastery and taking some meals there expected by most monks. At the visitation of Malmesbury Abbey in 1527 – a kind of special enquiry at which the abbot of Gloucester interviewed the monks about the performance of the abbot – one monk complained that the misericord was not supplied with decent cups for drinking. Awareness of the devious ways in which monks were avoiding the spirit while conforming to the letter of the *Rule* doubtless lies behind the ruling of Pope Benedict XII in his reform of monastic life in 1336, that no meat was to be eaten in dormitories. Greek Orthodox monastic rules, equally aware of such loopholes, often specified that food could only be eaten in the refectory.

It is easy for us to see this as a cynical attempt to outmanoeuvre the *Rule* for the sake of greed, and so that monks might live as they pleased rather than as they were supposed to. How can this apparent cynicism be explained? We must always bear in mind the social background of monks in the medieval Western world. In contrast with many of the early monks of the Egyptian and Syrian deserts, medieval monks tended to come from aristocratic, land-owning families. This is probably especially true of oblates, though what we know about Cistercians, Carthusians and other monks at reforming monasteries also bears this out. Hugh the Great of Cluny, for example, was a member of a prominent aristocratic family, and godfather to Emperor Henry IV; Peter the Venerable, his twelfth-century successor, was similarly aristocratic in origin; and Henry, bishop of Winchester, who had been a monk at Cluny, was the brother of the count of Blois and future king of England. Even Bernard of Clairvaux, though not quite so socially prominent, can be firmly regarded as 'knightly' – his brothers, uncle and cousins were all knights. Aelred, abbot of Rievaulx in the mid-twelfth century, had before his conversion to monasticism been steward at the court of the king of Scotland, and was related to the royal family;

and Norbert of Xanten, founder of the Premonstratensian Order, was similarly related to the Holy Roman Emperor. Monks known to have come from humble origins are few and far between. This means that most monks were comfortable with, and in many cases had grown up alongside, secular aristocrats. Their expectations and tastes, even in the cloister, were those of the aristocratic world.

Moreover, the aristocratic world – and even middle-class urban society – was by the twelfth century accustomed to a much more varied and comfortable diet than the sixth-century Italy for which Benedict had been legislating. Furthermore, a great monastery such as Cluny, Saint-Denis, Monte Cassino, St Albans or Westminster, was itself part of a social and political network. As such, monasteries often played host to important guests, including royalty (the early Capetian kings of France used to travel from one monastery to another so as to feed their households at the abbots' expense instead of their own). Provision for lavish eating was therefore often at hand, even if such banquets took place in the abbot's household rather than in the refectory.

Monks were not only aristocratic, they were also highly trained and educated, especially in the art of the critical understanding of texts. Interpreting scripture entailed mastery of methods of logical analysis and argument that, although opposed by some monks such as Bernard of Clairvaux, nevertheless took hold of the intellectual climate in many monasteries. Trained with such weaponry, it is not surprising that monks applied categories of analysis to their own guiding text, the *Rule of Benedict*. Arguments that might appear to us deliberate sophistry, such as the distinction between 'meat' and 'made with meat', came naturally as a result of such training. More important, however, was the understanding of what the monastic community as a whole meant. In 1336, Pope Benedict XII, who as a monk himself was noted for his reform of monasteries, ruled that no monastery should ever permit more than half the number of monks resident in the monastery at any one time to eat in any room other than the refectory. This enabled monasteries, even while openly permitting considerable laxity in observance, to claim that 'the community' was in fact observing the *Rule*. In order to understand how such an argument could have been acceptable, we first need to appreciate that Benedict's *Rule* envisioned the monastery as a single community rather than as a collective group of individuals. The *Rule* only made sense, indeed, if monks willingly denied their individual wills and identities to be absorbed into the community. It followed that the actions of individuals did not necessarily jeopardize the integrity of the community, for the whole was more than the sum of its constituent parts. Even if some monks were, therefore, absenting themselves from the refectory and eating meat, it did not invalidate the fact that, as long as vegetables and bread were served in the refectory, *the community* was observing the *Rule*. A similar logic underscored the observance of manual labour. Although by the twelfth century few monasteries really practised anything other than ritualized manual labour, the fact that it was done on certain occasions meant that the *Rule* was being observed.

We know a great deal about how and what monks at one English monastery, Westminster Abbey, ate in the later Middle Ages because the account rolls of the monks who filled the main offices in the monastery (the 'obedientaries') have survived. These accounts form the backbone of Barbara Harvey's detailed and vivid reconstruction of life in a late medieval monastery, *Living and Dying in England, 1100–1540*. What follows summarizes her work. In around 1500, the main meal at Westminster comprised pottage, a soup that might be made with oats and either vegetables or possibly fish or meat mixed into it. This served as a first course, and was then followed by the two daily dishes specified in the *Rule*, featuring vegetables or beans. Because of the way in which meat was interpreted, these might be rissoles made with meat, or meatballs, entrails, offal or, presumably, anything made with sausage meat or in a pie. A fourth dish, known as 'services', was provided as an extra pittance. On most days this was probably standard fare of the same kind as the ordinary dishes, but on saints' feast days, it might be something quite special, such as a game bird or freshwater fish. Since there were as many as seventy such feast days in the year, monks would have the chance to eat such luxuries about once every five days. On an average day at Westminster Abbey in around 1500, about 35 per cent of a monk's diet consisted of bread, 17 per cent meat and 6 per cent fish. Of the meat consumed by monks, 47 per cent was mutton or lamb, 35 per cent beef or veal, and 14 per cent pork, although at some other monasteries – Eynsham in Oxfordshire, and Shrewsbury, for example – pork was more popular. Eggs, milk and cheese accounted for another 8.5 per cent, suet (presumably in pies and puddings) 7 per cent, oatmeal a negligible 1 per cent, and, astonishingly, vegetables only half of 1 per cent. The remaining 25 per cent was taken in ale or wine. In Lent, the proportions of bread and ale rose to 45.5 per cent and 32.5 per cent respectively, but the main difference lay in the complete replacement of meat with fish, which accounted for 18 per cent of the diet. No dairy or suet was eaten at all, but, surprisingly, the proportion of vegetables did not rise to compensate for this; instead, dried fruit, which do not appear to have been eaten at all for most of the year, made up 2.5 per cent of the diet. The obvious conclusion we can draw is that, by the late Middle Ages, monks were no longer in any meaningful sense eating according to the demands of the *Rule*. Instead, they had adopted more or less the diet of aristocratic lay society.[9]

How did monasteries get away with such blatant abuses of the *Rule*? We have already noted the way that monasteries circumvented the *Rule* by using other rooms for eating. At Westminster, the misericord was first in use at some point between 1230 and 1270. It seems to have operated on the basis of a schedule, according to which monks took turns to eat there – and thus to eat roast or boiled meat quite openly – rather than in the refectory. Not only was the choice of food in the misericord not constrained by the *Rule*, but the prohibition on an evening meal between September and Easter could also be ignored. This meant, according to Barbara Harvey, that Westminster monks from the middle of the thirteenth century onward probably ate meat four times a week, and had

Stuffed eggs

Bernard of Clairvaux's *Apologia to the Abbot William* complains about the variety of ways in which eggs are served in monastic refectories, including 'stuffed eggs'. He may have been thinking of a dish such as this recipe, which I have adapted from the later Italian collection known as the *Libro di cucina*.

Hard boil eight eggs, then peel and slice in half. Spoon out the cooked yolks into a bowl and mash together, adding a whole raw egg. Add a pinch of marjoram, a few strands of saffron, half a teaspoon of ground cloves and a couple of ounces of grated pecorino cheese. When this mixture is smooth, spoon it back into the hard-boiled egg halves. Brown some butter in a frying pan, and very carefully sauté the egg halves on all sides in the butter for a few minutes. Serve with a bowl of verjuice on the side. This can be made with crab apples or an equal mixture of cider vinegar and water.

supper as well as dinner five or six times a week throughout the year. We should bear in mind that during this period, meat eating seems to have become more intensive throughout Europe, and there is far more evidence for the rearing of livestock and for the meat trade in general. This suggests that monks were simply copying the habits of the upper- and middle-class society from which most of them came.

Besides the misericord, there were two other places in which medieval monks might escape the rigours of the *Rule*. One was the infirmary, where Benedict had permitted meat to be eaten to enable sick monks to regain their strength. Special rules for convalescing monks were standard throughout the Byzantine world as well. In the typikon of the Byzantine monastery of Eleousa, founded on the Empire's Bulgarian border in the late eleventh century, sick monks were not fed meat but, in addition to the customary two dishes of vegetables and beans, they were provided with a third consisting of fish. In the later Middle Ages, the infirmary's dining room seems to have been a place to which anyone who could talk round the infirmarian resorted so as to enjoy a better meal. The other exception was the abbot's table. Benedict's *Rule* allowed the abbot to eat separately from the monks, and to keep his own table for entertaining guests and pilgrims. At great monasteries like Cluny, a separate household for the abbot, with his own dining room, developed from quite early on, and this was probably the pattern at most Western monasteries throughout the Middle Ages. In contrast, reform monasteries in the Byzantine world seem to have seen this as an abuse of cenobitic custom. The typikon of the monastery of Eleousa insisted that unless all monks, including the abbot, dined on the same food, the whole principle of cenobitism would be jeopardized. In this, Eleousa probably followed the ruling of the monastery of Theotokos Evergetis, founded in the suburbs of Constantinople in 1048–9, whose typikon became a standard model for new monasteries throughout the Empire. At the

Le Menagier de Paris's almond milk soup

This delicate soup is ideal for the infirmary, but can also be enjoyed by healthy monks.

Bring a pot of water containing two onions to the boil. Meanwhile blanch about 300 grams of almonds in boiling water to soften the skins; leave to cool and peel. After the water has boiled for about 20 minutes, take out the onions and set aside, retaining the water. Next, pound the almonds in a large mortar or food processor, adding most of the water used to cook the onions. Strain the liquid through a muslin cloth to produce a fine milky liquid. Next fry the onions gently in butter. Once the onions are golden brown, add them to the almond milk. Serve with croutons or toast.

monastery of Makhairas in Cyprus, founded in the middle of the twelfth century, the abbot dined separately when there were distinguished visitors to entertain during a period of fast, notably Lent – but the monks had to keep to their fast. At the English Benedictine monastery of Evesham, one of the many complaints made about the abbot Roger de Norrys, in the early thirteenth century, was that he refused to eat in the refectory with the other monks.[10]

In monasteries where distinctions between the abbot's table and the refectory were common, monks might be invited to dine with the abbot on occasion. Anselm, who as archbishop of Canterbury was also abbot of Christ Church, the monastic community that staffed the cathedral, used invitations to the abbot's table as a means of teaching select groups of monks. At the abbot's table, not only was the normal rule of silence waived, but the food served was also very different because of the need to cater for guests.[11] At Bury St Edmunds in the late twelfth century, Abbot Samson and his guests were typically served four courses at dinner, which might include venison or some other such rich meat. Abbot Samson was particularly concerned not to appear to be niggardly in his hospitality, even though the abbey was in serious financial trouble when he became abbot. In order to be able to provide for guests, he kept his own deer parks stocked with game animals and ponds full of fish, though his biographer assures us that he never saw the abbot himself touch venison.

Bishop Hugh of Lincoln was a younger contemporary of Samson who had been a Carthusian monk before his elevation to the bishopric. Although as bishop he was required to maintain a stately household and to feed a number of people, like Samson he himself stuck to a strict monastic diet, refraining from meat. Abbot Samson appears to have been a man of strict self-discipline, for although surrounded by culinary delicacies, his favourite food was fresh milk and honey. If he did not like a dish served to him, he did not send it back and ask for a replacement, but simply left it untouched. Jocelyn of Brakelond, the abbot's biographer, says that when he was a novice taking his turn at serving duties, he once tried to test him by putting in front of Samson a dish that was evidently so awful that everybody else had refused to touch it. Samson pretended not to see it, and Jocelyn, thinking better of his trick, took it away and replaced it with a different one, whereupon Samson told him off for trying to improve the meal unnecessarily. At the other end of the spectrum of abbatial hospitality is the feast of roast lamb served to the pope and his household at tables set up in the cloister, as guests of the monastery of Saint-Denis at Easter in 1132.[12]

Whatever the explanations for monasteries becoming more relaxed in their eating habits, there is no doubt that contemporaries noticed and were often unimpressed by it. This kind of contemporary criticism seems to have become widespread by the time of the Dissolution of the monasteries, and contributed to the later mythology of dissolute feasting monks. In fact, many monasteries were by the sixteenth century very impoverished, as the visitation records of the 1530s show. Protestant historians of the seventeenth century and beyond had clear reasons, however, for wanting to portray the later medieval monks as creatures of indolence and luxury. A good example is the story told in Thomas Fuller's *History of the British Church* (1655), in which Henry VIII visits Reading Abbey in disguise and is entertained as a simple guest by the abbot. He puts away with gusto a sirloin steak, but the abbot regrets that his digestion does not allow him to join his guest, and explains that he can only manage rabbit or chicken. A few weeks later the abbot is summoned to London and peremptorily imprisoned in the Tower, where he is fed on bread and water for several days. One day, instead of his usual rations, a sirloin steak is put in front of him, and he falls on it with relish – whereupon King Henry leaps out from his hiding place and demands that the abbot pay him £100 as a fee for having cured him of his digestive troubles.

ALMS AND THE POOR

The last stage of the journey of monastic food was from the table to the almoner's gate. Benedict's *Rule*, imitating what had already become standard practice in monastic communities, specified that leftover uneaten food was to be distributed in alms to the poor who came to the monastery gates to receive it. This stipulation is also found in Byzantine typika from the earliest days and repeated in reforming rules from the eleventh century onward. The Evergetis typikon adjured monks that no pauper seeking alms was to be turned away from the gate of the monastery empty-handed. Reforming monasteries in the eleventh and twelfth centuries trying to emulate the original monastic way of life seized on this as a core value of the profession. At the new reforming community of Obazine, in the forests of Limousin in western France, the founder, Stephen, distributed leftover food to any paupers who came to the door, but if there was no one at the door, he kept the leftovers to mix with the food to be cooked the next day.

Hospitality to the poor, to be distinguished from the feeding of guests, was one of the chief social duties of monasteries in both Eastern and Western traditions. However, the initial principle of doling out uneaten food to the poor developed into something subtly different. Rather than simply giving out what was left over, monasteries began to make special doles to the poor. This, obviously, necessitated preparing extra food in the first place. Since all food given to the poor had to come from the surplus of the monks' own table, the kitchen staff must have had to deliberately overestimate the amount of food needed to ensure that leftovers were available. At Cluny in the twelfth century, twelve three-pound loaves of bread were distributed at the almonry door daily to the paupers of the town. On some days, however, the dole was spectacularly increased. Every Maundy Thursday, the same number of poor men as there were monks in the abbey were fed with the same food as the monks themselves. Given that there were about 300 monks at Cluny by the 1120s, this was a substantial commitment. It was surpassed, however, by the feast specially cooked and served on Quinquagesima Sunday, when all the poor who turned up at the monastery gate were given a meal of salt pork. It has been calculated that in 1085 this meant the slaughter and cooking of 250 pigs. William of Malmesbury, writing in the 1130s, calculated that Reading Abbey gave away more food than it consumed. Norwich Cathedral priory donated 1,500 quarts of malt and 800 of wheat in one year.

The custom of serving surplus food inevitably also led to the preparation of food that was never intended for monks to eat. Samson of Bury St Edmunds used to exploit this loophole regularly. Although he never ate meat himself, Samson always insisted on having at least one meat dish served at his table, even if he had no guests on that day, so that he could have good food to give to the poor. Samson wanted to ensure that those who came to the abbey gates for alms might sometimes be given food they can hardly ever have hoped to taste. But the system could also lead to abuses of the system. An unscrupulous monk or monastery servant could secretly steal food and sell it for his own profit, without appearing to be defrauding the monastery. The General Chapter of the English Benedictines, recognizing the danger, passed a regulation in 1277 to prohibit the pilfering of leftovers before they reached the almoner. Even so, a specific prohibition on selling food prepared in a monastery had to be repeated in 1363, in a series of articles prepared for the regular visitation of monasteries, so the practice seems to have been continuing. In the later Middle Ages, some Benedictine monasteries took a further step in providing for the poor by housing as well as feeding almsmen. These people were fed from the uneaten portions of the food served in the refectory. Given that so many monks regularly ate in the misericord or elsewhere, this system ought to have meant that quite a lot of food was available for the almsmen. In 1417, however, the six resident Westminster almsmen petitioned the abbot for an extra 2d to be spent daily on them because on fast days, when the refectory was likely to be full, they could not be sure of getting anything to eat. Twopence probably bought a little less than a pound of fairly cheap fish such as herring for each almsman.

The complexities of providing the daily nutritional needs of a large community that was, in principle, self-sufficient meant inevitably that monasteries developed institutionally in ways that took them far from the ideals of the early monks. Laconic entries in English monastic chronicles, such as the record of a thief breaking into the abbot of Dunstable's pig-byre and killing fourteen pigs in 1245, take us into a world in which monasteries were major land-owning corporations. By around 1200, most large monasteries were going concerns. The obedientaries, including the cellarer, had to render separate accounts of income and expenditure, and their operations were funded by manors that they had to run profitably if they were to be able to meet the needs of the monks.

This may be a far cry from the monk in Sulpicius Severus' story with which this chapter opened, growing his grain in a patch of Egyptian sand. But, even in the early days of cenobitic monasticism in Egypt, something similar, albeit less well developed, operated at Pachomius' monasteries. Teams of monks were sent out regularly armed with implements for planting, hoeing and harvesting, and monasteries kept herds of cattle and buffalo for milk and cheese. The difference between Pachomius' monasteries in the desert of Upper Egypt, and the lush manors and gardens of English medieval monasteries, cannot necessarily be explained by changes in spirituality or observance. It must be sought instead in the huge social and economic changes that characterized Europe and the Mediterranean in the period between the eleventh and fifteenth centuries. In the next chapter we will examine the wider social context of eating and cooking in the medieval world.

Chapter Six

Medieval diets – the food landscape

TYPICAL MEDIEVAL DIETS

Writing about the food eaten by monks and monastic communities in antiquity and the Middle Ages raises obvious questions of comparison. How did the standard monastic fare contrast, if at all, with what was eaten in secular households and families? I have already hinted in one or two anecdotes concerning solitary monks that the kind of abstinence regarded as so virtuous by monks was in fact a necessity for many people living on the margins of populated society.

When we look at the basic food available even to a monastery on the edges of the desert, the impression we get is one of solid comfort, if not plenty. The *Rule of Pachomius* mentions the following kinds of foods, either grown or produced in the monastery or imported: beans, lentils, cabbages, olives (and olive oil), parsley, dates, leeks, onions, garlic, spinach, apples, figs, carobs, nuts, buffalo milk, cheese, wheat, palm flour, salt and fish. With regional variations, this probably conforms closely to the standard foods eaten across the Mediterranean during most of the first millennium AD. This diet is characterized by a heavy reliance on fish and bread, beans and other pulses, and the *allium* family of vegetables. Towards the end of the thirteenth century, a Frankish inhabitant of the kingdom of Jerusalem listed the plants that were native to his country, and which could be grown and harvested with very little effort, as wild fennel, rue, salvia (sage), oranges, lemons and citrons, grapes, figs, olives, honey, peppers, cucumbers and prickly pears. Sugar cane was also grown in large quantities, though it needed intensive efforts to refine it to an edible state. Documents from southern Italian monasteries show that the basic diet revolved around the foods that were grown or gathered in the region: wheat, millet, wine, apples, figs, chestnuts, olives, greens including leeks and chard, beans and chickpeas. As we have seen in the previous chapter, in medieval northern Europe, beans and peas, cereals, leafy green plants such as the kale family, and leeks, onions and garlic dominated the daily diet. We can add to this list the standard orchard fruit: apples, pears and nuts, in place of the Mediterranean standard of olives, figs and grapes.

Some important factors must be borne in mind when we think about what medieval people ate. Naturally, there was always a difference between what the elites at the top of society could afford to eat and the diet of the vast majority of the population. Town-dwellers and those who could afford to buy imported food always had access to a more varied diet. However, over the thousand years or so commonly taken to constitute the Middle Ages, there are really two distinct, but not easily defined, periods of time. Between about the sixth century and the year 1000 or 1100, the main difference between the diet of the wealthy and the poor was probably largely one of quantity. From about 1100, however, and certainly from 1200 onward, the extension of trade patterns and the development of new markets meant that for those who could afford it, almost any kind of food was available, at a price. One reason for the difference in diet was that a revolution in agriculture seems to have taken place around the year AD 1000. The use of heavy draught horses to pull ploughs in place of oxen meant that more land could be ploughed in a shorter time. At the same time, the introduction of windmills made the milling of grain more efficient than ever before. More efficient techniques meant that more food could be grown, which in turn meant that more people could be fed. Consequently the European population grew in the eleventh century, probably for the first time since the days of the Roman Empire.

Naturally, this did not mean that everyone ate rich or varied diets. In regions where agricultural soils were poor, or where the environment was mountainous, such as southern Italy and Greece, the diet must often have been desperately limited. At times of famine, such as resulted from the very poor harvests recorded in some years of the early fourteenth century throughout Europe, everyone suffered. Nevertheless, the current opinion among historical anthropologists seems to be that high rates of mortality in Europe's past were generally caused by epidemics rather than poor nutritional factors. It has been suggested that 2,000 calories per day was an adequate intake per person in pre-industrial societies. This must have been relatively easy to obtain in most of the Mediterranean and Western Europe, although in some areas it may have meant eating large quantities of cereals. Deficiency in vitamin intake – especially E and B – was likely to have been a greater problem than low calorific intake. However, even in poor areas, a relative lack of protein provided by meat was compensated by high intake of vitamins. The Neapolitans were known as *mangiafolie* – 'leaf-eaters' – because of their high intake of greenstuff. This seems to have been deliberately cultivated since the growing of 'leaves' appears frequently in medieval land documents from Naples.

The wealthiest spent huge amounts on themselves and their households. Medieval society, especially from the thirteenth century onward, was – not unlike our own – one of conspicuous consumption. Spending more than one could really afford was a way for the aristocracy to show their power to potential rivals – even if the message thus conveyed was deceptive. Noble and knightly families were quite prepared to spend beyond their means to improve their homes, to make a splash with lavish entertainments and clothes, to maintain households employing large numbers of servants, retainers and hangers-on, and on food. Spending on food and drink made up the biggest expenditure in large and wealthy households. This could amount to as much as half of the total income in quite a small knight's household. Battle Abbey seems to have been more or less typical of wealthy monasteries in spending almost two-thirds of its income on food, though in a comparable secular household – that of an earl rather than a simple knight – the figure seems to have come to less than 50 per cent. Naturally, the amounts spent on certain kinds of food and drink varied the higher up the social scale one went. An earl might spend 20 per cent of his total food budget on wine, while a simple knight spent closer to 2 per cent. Similarly, the duke of Buckingham spent 7 per cent of his income on spices, whereas Thomas of Berkeley, a rich Gloucestershire baron, spent only 3 per cent. Money spent on spices, the most expensive single kind of food on the market, was a demonstration of one's spending power, no less than adding a new wing to a castle or manor house. This was true not only in the West, but also in the eastern Mediterranean. The accounts of middle-class Levantine families from the thirteenth century show that they spent as much on spices as on meat.

For the most part, however, comparisons of proportions of expenditure in different aristocratic households in the fourteenth and fifteenth centuries show that, whatever the range of income, households spent roughly the same proportions on the same kinds of foods. The biggest item of expenditure was always meat and fish (as much as 50 per cent of the total food budget of the duke of Gloucester), followed by bread and ale. We can infer from this that, although great households kept livestock and herds to slaughter for meat, and even maintained deer parks for game, increasingly they bought what they ate rather than rearing it themselves. Dairy produce and fresh vegetables and fruit made up negligible amounts, probably because much of these were produced or grown within the household.[1]

In secular, as in monastic households, bread was a staple part of the daily diet. Bread was probably eaten with every meal, and just as a daily allocation of bread was provided for monks according to the *Rule of Benedict*, so also monastic and secular households alike provided set amounts of daily bread for their servants. Bread also served as a 'trencher', or plate, for poorer families or for servants and lower employees in great households. The fact that monks ate from dishes was a mark of their largely aristocratic background. There were huge differences across the medieval world in the type of grain used to produce bread, but everyone, from great lords to peasants, probably ate bread every day. The wealthy ate white bread, made from refined wheat. In parts of Europe and the Mediterranean where wheat was plentiful, eating white bread was not necessarily such a mark of status, but in much of Europe, white bread was eaten only by those who could afford it.

White bread was expensive, partly because in order to produce it, one had to mill off a proportion of the bran from the grain. The bran could then be fed to animals, so it was not wasted, but the process obviously demanded a higher amount of grain in the first place in order to make the required quantity of bread. Eating mixed grain was a sign of particular abstinence in the early monastic tradition. Hilarion was noted for eating only barley bread between the ages of thirty-one and thirty-five. A number of other grains could be substituted for wheat, depending on what cereals grew locally: barley, rye, even ground beans. Bolton Abbey, for example, provided loaves of 'gruel bread', made of rye, barley and beans, for its servants. The Cistercian Statutes of 1134, however, insisted that the bread eaten by the monks should be of whole bran rather than refined white wheat, or rye in places where that grain was more common. Maslin bread, a mixture of wheat and rye grains, was sometimes used in place of plates at the table.

Wealthy and poor alike consumed large quantities of cereals, both in the form of bread and ale. The staple food of the poor in much of Western Europe, as testified by Piers Plowman, was pottage. What exactly this comprised has divided opinions among food historians. Some maintain that it was a cereal-based dish made from a mixture of oats and pulses, similar to pease pudding, and thus a rather stodgy food heavy with protein and starch. The current view, however, inclines to see it rather as a thin broth with vegetables – the ubiquitous leeks and onions, and seasonal green-stuff such as kale and cabbage, or peas and beans – that might be enriched with scraps of meat if available.[2] This makes it much more akin to the daily soup of Byzantine monasteries, and probably also to what was served in Benedictine monasteries. It is only natural that the staple food served to monks should have been a dish well known to everyone as the basic food of the poorer classes everywhere in Europe. Precisely because most monks, at least in Western Europe, did not come from this social class, the fact that they ate it as their daily staple carried a particular symbolic value. Because the materials for such a dish are so mundane, and would have been supplied by the kitchen garden, it is almost untraceable in the surviving accounts of households. But the greater the household, the more servants had to be fed, and pottage, accompanied by bread, was probably cooked and served in most large kitchens as well as peasant households every day. One theory is that, in secular households and monasteries alike, pottage formed a standard first course, after which, in wealthy households and monasteries, more substantial dishes would follow.

What really distinguished the tables of the great were the meat and fish served at them. Both the quantities and variety are staggering. Besides beef, pork, mutton, lamb and venison, a whole range of game birds and animals found their way to aristocratic tables: coney, rabbit, partridge, pheasant, goose, duck, peacock, heron and swan. In the sixteenth century, the chronicler Ralph Hollinshed declared that the English nobility ate a greater variety of meat than any other nation. Birds were eaten indiscriminately – plovers, pigeons, quail, snipe, woodcock, even sparrows. There are even recipes for beaver, bear and porpoise – the latter classified as fish and therefore perfectly legitimate during fasts. 'Fish' also included all manner of shellfish: crab, crayfish, lobster, mussels, oysters, scallops, whelks and prawns. Among what we would properly call fish, almost every species that swam can be found in medieval cookery books: besides the cod, haddock, hake, bream, mackerel, salmon and halibut familiar to us, they ate carp, conger eels, dace, dogfish, gurnard, lamprey, ling, loach, luce, perch, pickerel, pike, sole, sturgeon, swordfish, tench and turbot.

Why such variety and deliberate exoticism? Partly it was to show off. Medieval aristocratic culture gloried in ostentation and spectacle, and feasts provided opportunities to create lavish fantasies out of food. Cooks were encouraged to demonstrate their skills to appreciative audiences for whom the banquet was a spectacle in which the visual was almost as important as the sensory. Cooks liked to create illusions with food. Food might be sculpted into different shapes, or disguised as something quite different to what it really was. Dried fruit were disguised in batter and roasted to resemble haslet, the entrails of a boar; meatballs, also coated with batter, were rolled in chopped parsley to look like apples. But of course, even aristocratic households did not hold banquets every day. Probably a more fundamental reason for the variety of meat and fishes eaten was that the greater the household, the larger the number of people that had to be fed daily. As with food that was grown, so also the availability of livestock was seasonal. At times when fresh meat might not be so readily available, either from the household's own supplies or from butchers, cooks and cellarers had to be resourceful in order to keep households fed, and this meant using as much of every animal as was edible. This is also the reason why so many recipes were developed for entrails and offal, which seem to have been quite acceptable, even to aristocratic tastes.

Aristocratic households in the later Middle Ages seem to have eaten more meat than had been the case in earlier centuries. It is difficult to be certain, because the accounts that survive for some households from the thirteenth century onward have no counter-parts from earlier periods. However, historians have shown that there was more pasture land available for great estates, especially after the population suffered a dramatic decline in the fourteenth century – the Black Death reduced the population of the whole of Europe by between a third and a half over the course of a genera-tion in the middle of that century. One result of this was that less food was needed, and this in turn meant that more arable land could be given over to pasture for livestock – and thus, that those who survived had more meat to eat.

Of the main varieties of meat eaten, beef was the most popular. In the household of the Lincolnshire knight Sir William Skipworth, forty-nine beef cattle were slaughtered for food in 1467–8; this

Steamed beef

This recipe, like the next two, is adapted from *The Forme of Cury*. You will need a large jar that can be secured tightly at the top. Chop a kilo of stewing steak or shin of beef into small bite-sized pieces. Put the pieces of beef into the jar with a large onion, chopped fine. Add half a teaspoon each of whole cloves and ground mace, and a small handful of currants or raisins. Fill to the top with red wine. Place a disc of greaseproof paper over the top of the jar, secure with string, and place a small cloth over this. The important point is to ensure that no liquid can get in or out of the jar. Put the jar in a large saucepan half full of water; bring the water slowly to the boil, then simmer until the meat is cooked. The length of time this takes will vary depending on the size and shape of the jar, but check after about 45 minutes of simmering.

compares with seventy-four sheep and around the same number of pigs. Given the relative proportions of meat to weight, this means beef amounted to three-quarters of all the meat eaten in the household. Having said that, this is a large figure, and the average number for most aristocratic households was probably closer to half. In contrast, the proportion of beef to other meats eaten by the Cistercians of Beaulieu Abbey in the late thirteenth century was less than one sixth. Non-monastic noble households, whether headed by a bishop or a secular lord, were often on the move from one estate to another, so that the reserves of livestock could be eaten in one before moving on to another. Even so, beef and other meats were often bought on the open market to supplement the livestock raised on estates. It is more difficult to assess the importance of game in the meat diet, because deer was hunted in parks or forests, and although these game reserves were privately owned, few records were kept of how many animals were killed or how much of the meat was eaten. It has been estimated that venison amounted to about 10 per cent of the meat of an earl's household, but some actual figures put the amount even lower. We must remember, however, that the significance of venison lay as much in the ritual of hunting that surrounded it as in the nutrition it provided.

There can be no doubt that the wealthy had both a greater variety of food and larger amounts, especially of meat and fish, in the period from the thirteenth century onward. This was the great age of ceremonial banquets and of the art of cookery, celebrated in a number of recipe books that still survive. It was also the age of spices and exotic ingredients from the ends of the earth. To understand why food habits and eating improved so dramatically in this period, we must first look at how European society itself underwent a profound series of changes, beginning after the millennium of AD 1000.

EUROPE, TRADE AND THE FOOD ECONOMY

The Roman Empire had turned the Mediterranean Sea into a very large lake. The *pax romana* meant that goods and people could be moved with relative ease, depending on the season. For most of the year, it was much easier to transport goods across the Mediterranean by ship than by roads in the interior of the Empire. Ships carried not only long-distance trade from one end of the Empire to the other, but also did the more important short-hop journeys, such as transporting goods from northern to southern Italy. When this kind of activity slowed down, we can be fairly sure that the Empire was, for all practical purposes, coming to an end. Of course, the question that cannot be answered with any certainty is in what generation the difference became obvious. What we can say is that in the sixth century both short- and long-distance trade are very noticeable in the archaeological record, whereas by the end of the seventh century, both archaeological and literary evidence suggest that trade patterns were becoming restricted. The presence of Syrian merchants in Marseilles, for example, aroused intense curiosity in seventh-century Gaul, whereas a couple of hundred years earlier it would have been unremarkable.

For a period of about five or six hundred years after long-distance trade dried up, what people ate was constrained by where they lived. Of course, this continued to be true to a degree even after the extension of trade routes once again in the twelfth century. To some extent it is still the case today, though now it is more a matter of taste and local identity than of necessity. But the availability of a greater variety of foods through the development of new markets is one of the most distinctive features of the period after about 1100 or 1200; and once availability was assured, taste followed. Why new markets arose in Europe when they did is not a simple matter, although the eleventh century is recognized as being the crucial time in the development of a society that was much closer to the one in which we still live, with distinct nation states, the rule of law and stable political institutions.

Part of the reason for the profound changes between about AD 1000 and 1100 is that Europe was no longer threatened by external invasion. The first millennium had seen waves of invasion, immigration and new settlement across the continent. From the south and east, the Arabs spread rapidly across the former Roman provinces of North Africa and Spain, colonized the Mediterranean islands from Cyprus to the Balearics, and raided the southern French and Italian coastlines. They even sacked Rome in the tenth century. From Scandinavia, the Vikings first ravaged and then settled in Britain, Ireland and northern France, while from the steppes of central Asia came perhaps the most terrifying threat of all: the nomadic Magyar horsemen. For a hundred and fifty years from about AD 800 onwards, most of Western Europe suffered at least the fear, if not the reality, of raids and sometimes invasion from one of these enemies of civilization. But from the middle of the tenth century, the threat gradually diminished as strong rulers asserted themselves once again in Europe. A hundred years later, the millennium had passed without the disasters that some learned clerics had forseen, and although Europe was far from peaceful, it was beginning to develop stable institutions of government.

Monasteries, places of order, spiritual routine and learning, were among the most important of these, and they had a strong influence on society at large. Governments depended on monasteries because they were repositories of learning, memory and – at least, in principle – piety. Not only kings and other secular rulers, but also the newly burgeoning papal government, needed the advice and spiritual authority provided by monasteries. By about 1100, papal government was dominated by monks, and for three successive generations most popes had themselves been monks. Kings also relied on monks, not least because monasteries were such large landowners that they were politically important. Like secular landowners, monasteries owed dues and services on their lands, and for kings, the most important of these was military service in the form of soldiers for the feudal levy. In the new European order, monasteries were at the heart of society. The stability that accompanied the development of strong institutions also made possible quicker and more secure communication across Europe, and more travel than ever before.

Travel, both local and across long distances, lay at the heart of good order. Rulers could only govern distant provinces if they could be there in person or send representatives. It would not be exaggerating to say that the ability to communicate through travel was the key to the transformation of Europe in the eleventh and twelfth centuries from inchoate local principalities to centralized government. This applied to the Church as well as to states. Popes began to issue instructions and decrees, through bulls and encyclicals, which they could now expect to be carried out by bishops. The twelfth century, in consequence, saw the very rapid growth of papal administration as the pope became the centre of the Church in actuality as well as theory. Bishops and monasteries who were unsure of what course of action to take, or who wanted to claim exemptions or bring a case in canon law, had to travel to Rome to take their case to the papal court. Only when such frequent travel was possible could a ruler, whether a king or a pope, really be at the centre of government. By about 1200, the roads of Europe must have been full of couriers, messengers, emissaries and legates criss-crossing the continent bearing dispatches, letters and instructions from one court to another.

More secure travel not only meant that governments worked more effectively, but also that there were more opportunities for trade. At a local and regional level, more markets were created within Europe that attracted merchants from longer distances. Navigable rivers, roads and bridges, and coastal navigation, brought a greater range of goods, including food, to more people. By the thirteenth century, for example, saltwater fish could be had almost anywhere in England, even if it had to be salted or preserved for transport to areas far from coasts. Long-distance trade also revived, and trade went hand-in-hand with another form of travel: overseas conquest and colonization. It is no coincidence that around the same time as European society began to develop stronger internal institutions, it also began to expand outwards and to settle in new areas. In part, this was the result of missionary activity and conversion: Scandinavia and Hungary both adopted Christianity in the early eleventh century, and thus became part of the new European order, and from Saxony, German settlers pushed east across the Elbe into the coastal plains of Poland. To the south, the Christian kingdoms of northern Spain, tiny but with fast-increasing populations, began to conquer the Moorish heartland of the peninsula. The Italian cities of Amalfi, Genoa, Pisa and Venice sent ships to trade with North Africa, Egypt and Constantinople. The Normans epitomized the new confidence of Western Europe. Only a hundred and fifty years after exchanging Scandinavia's fjords for the green pastures of northern France, they were on the move again: Normans settled in masterless southern Italy and invaded Muslim Sicily; they conquered and settled in England and Wales; and at the end of the eleventh century, they took part in the great enterprise of conquest and colonization in the Near East that we know as the First Crusade.

Conquest and colonization in the Mediterranean was only possible with command of the seas. This, in turn, meant more opportunities for trade in southern waters. It was the Italian maritime cities that first took advantage of the new situation created by military conquest and colonization. The Venetians and Genoese were quite prepared to help in the conquest of the great ports of the Levant by the crusaders, but only for a price. Whereas knights who took the cross and decided to stay in the East wanted fiefs on which to settle and build new livelihoods, the Italians wanted trading concessions. After their help in the capture of Tyre in 1123, for example, the Venetians agreed a contract with the kingdom of Jerusalem that effectively granted them a whole quarter of the city for themselves, as Venetian territory. Here they could build warehouses, establish markets, and exploit the new possibilities of trade with their Syrian counterparts. From Damascus and Baghdad came silks, glass, spices and other luxury goods, while from the west the Italians brought the mundane, but more essential, iron and timber. Over time, quarters such as this became Italian enclaves, in which the Genoese or Venetians could build their own churches and palaces, and even apply the laws of their own cities. Trade was not only from Italy to the Levant, for ships could put in at various ports on the way and take advantage of local trading patterns. A Venetian ship might, en route for the East, pick up cargoes on the Dalmatian coast and trade them for different goods in Greece, before sailing on for Cyprus and their ultimate destination. The profits from Mediterranean trade were immense, and as Eastern goods became more familiar in the West, taste was stimulated for more. By the later Middle Ages it was not only the nobility that could afford and demanded luxury goods, but the new urban middle classes. Standards of living all over Europe rose because of the ready availability of goods that had once been considered rarities.

Among the Eastern goods that became so familiar was a new range of foods. With new foods came a revolution in taste. It was not so much new foods themselves that made the journey from east to west, for most of the basic foodstuffs grown and reared in the East and West were similar if not identical. As we have seen, a heavy reliance on beans, leeks, onions, garlic and cereal crops was characteristic of cultivation across the whole of Europe and the Mediterranean, and the main differences were in the kinds of herbs indigenous to different regions. The missing ingredient that the East could supply to the West, however, was spices.

SPICES AND COOKING

The West's taste for spices in cooking was certainly not new. We know that the Romans traded extensively in spices with the East, but the only surviving cookery book from the ancient world, by Apicius, does not make much use of them. Pepper, ginger, cinnamon, mace, nutmeg, bettle and musk appear in the sources – but not, we may say, in the sauces. Perhaps the Romans tended to use spices more as drugs and cosmetics than in their food. Medieval recipes, however, call for spices with almost monotonous consistency, and in ways that the Romans had not tried. Almonds, for example, were known to Apicius mainly as a garnish for dishes, but in European recipes from the thirteenth century onward, ground almonds appear as a thickener for sauces. Already by the twelfth century, the monastic reformer Bernard of Clairvaux was using the taste for spicy food as a mark of all that was degenerate in cooking. Spices, he thought, not only stimulated the appetite so that one wanted more, they also promoted lust. In contrast, plain unadorned food served the purpose of simply filling the body.

The main spices used in medieval cooking seem to have been cinnamon, mace, cloves, pepper and ginger. Coriander and cumin were also known, though they seem to have been more prevalent in Italian cookery than in French or English. Saffron was very highly regarded, perhaps as much for its colour as for its taste: the golden colour it imparted was a way of making food appear even more extravagant. Because of its great expense, saffron was imported only in small quantities, but by the end of the Middle Ages it was being grown successfully in the West – hence, for example, the name Saffron Walden. Sugar may also be included with the spices, since it was treated in much the same way: both in cooking and for sprinkling on food. Sugar was in fact less exotic than many other spices, since it never had to travel such long distances or pass through the hands of so many middle men. Sugar cane was one of the major industries of the crusader kingdom of Jerusalem in the twelfth and thirteenth centuries, where it grew very well in the hot and humid climate of the Jordan Valley near Jericho. Sugar-refining plants from the thirteenth century have also been excavated near the coastal town of Acre. Because of easy access to slave labour, from the subject Muslims under crusader rule, the industry required to extract the essential substance from the cane could be established on site, and the finished product exported to the West. It is a fallacy to suppose, as many people have, that sugar was a rarity and that honey was the main sweetener in medieval cooking.

Spices arrived in the West in different forms. Sometimes accounts recording their purchase speak simply of 'powders', which may mean that they were already pre-mixed, like modern curry powder. Some recipes expected whole spices, especially cloves, while others called for them in a variety of forms: fine or coarse ground, in cakes, in crystalline form (especially ginger) or even as a liquid, which was achieved by distillation in vinegar. There were also different types or grades of many spices: ginger might be specified as 'colombyne' or 'magdelyne', for example.

The taste for spices shows how far European medieval cooking was influenced by Arab cuisine. The similarities and borrowings in European recipes from Arabic writing about food are very marked. This does not mean, of course, that European cooks read Arabic books on cooking, but that the cuisine itself followed trade routes. Italian and French merchants in Levantine ports, pilgrims to the Holy Land and settlers in the East were all exposed to the local cuisine. The Arab knight Usama ibn Munqidh tells in his memoirs an anecdote about a Frankish crusader who had settled in Antioch and adopted Eastern ways to the extent of keeping an Egyptian cook,

avoiding pork and only eating halal meat.[3] Nevertheless, it is striking that books on cookery begin to appear in the West at the end of
the thirteenth century, when very little interest had previously been
shown in writing down recipes or comparing techniques of cooking. It may not be coincidental that the thirteenth century also saw
the production of Arabic texts on cooking and food. A Sicilian text,
the *Book of Cooking*, also from the thirteenth century, incorporates a
number of Arabic words in its recipes, and in general owes a debt
to Arabic styles of cooking. The reliance on spices was, therefore,
part of a general cultural taste for a style of living influenced by a
Middle Eastern and specifically Arabic aesthetic. Above all, however, spices meant wealth. To be able not merely to use spices in
the cooking process, but also sprinkled liberally over food, or even
between dishes on the table, signalled the host's access to markets
and his or her ability to pay exorbitant prices.

Before we look more specifically at some medieval recipes to
see the effects of this interest in spices, it is worth laying to rest
one particular myth about medieval cuisine. It has often been said
that one reason for the heavy use of spices was to disguise the
taste of bad or spoiled meat. It is puzzling why this belief should
have become so prevalent, unless from a general assumption that
people in the Middle Ages either knew no better than to eat bad
meat or were unable to supply themselves with fresh food. This
is misguided on several grounds. For one thing, in most medieval
recipes, quantities are not given, so although we know that large
amounts of spices were purchased, we do not know in most cases
how much was called for in specific recipes. A recipe for stewed
chicken, for example, requires the cook to simmer the bird in a
half-and-half mixture of broth and wine with cloves, mace, pepper
and cinnamon, but without saying how much of each spice was
to be used. It is true that some recipes specify a large amount; for
example, the fourteenth-century cookbook known as the *Libro di
cucina* has a recipe for a dish for twelve people which asks for two
ounces of mixed spices. This is a surprising amount, but on the
other hand, other recipes specify a pinch or touch only. It is thus

difficult to say with confidence that the spices were intended to disguise the taste of the meat.

Another problem with the theory is that the technologies of sourcing, preparing, and preserving meat were really no less advanced in the Middle Ages than in classical antiquity, when no such imputation is held. There is no reason to suppose that medieval people did not have access to fresh meat. Although it is probably true that most beef cattle were slaughtered before the winter months, when the lack of pasture made it more expensive to feed them, the traditional time for killing pigs was November, and in its various forms meat from the pig could be made to last until Lent. Then there was venison and other game, which were at their best in the autumn, and poultry and birds could be had for most of the year. Besides this, techniques for preserving meat and fish, either by salting or smoking, were well known throughout Europe. Spices, therefore, were eaten because people had developed a taste for them, and because that taste said something about their social status, not because they had to cover up bad food. The taste for spices could also be exploited. A physician in Salerno, the south Italian city pre-eminent in Europe for its medical school, recommended, with clear-headed cynicism, that pharmacists should use as many rich and exotic spices as possible to make medicines for the rich, on the grounds that they equated expense with efficacy, while for the poor, ordinary 'simples' made from one or two herbal ingredients would do just as well.

MEDIEVAL RECIPES

The earliest medieval cookbooks date from the late thirteenth century. Two manuscripts written in the French that was spoken in England around this period contain the first English recipes known to us. They contain about thirty recipes each, with some overlap between them. They include food and spiced wine, and cover a range of dishes, some rather humble, such as broths and flavoured pottages, and others rather fancier. Some are quite recognizable and show that basic techniques have not changed over the centuries: the recipe for pancakes, for example, could almost have been written for use today. Some striking features of the recipes as a collection stand out. One is the giving of nicknames to dishes. This reflects the liking for making one kind of food look like quite a different food. A dish called 'oranges', for example, turns out to be minced pork meatballs roasted over the fire and sprinkled with sugar. 'Nag's tail' is made from pigs' trotters and ears, cooked in wine, roasted over the fire and then simmered with onions and spices. One recipe for 'Turk's head' is an eel pie, while another dish with the same name is a haggis made with minced chicken, pork and spices cooked in a pig's stomach; yet another is a rabbit and chicken pie.[4]

A more significant feature of the collection is the obvious influence of the Mediterranean. A number of recipes either have an Eastern origin or are named for a dish that must have come from the eastern Mediterranean. 'Syrian food', for example, which can be white, yellow or green, is made from capon and rice. In the white version, the bird is set to boil with rice flour in a mixture of white wine and almond milk, to which ginger and sugar have been added; when the dish has cooled and set, pomegranate seeds are sprinkled on top. To make it green, substitute parsley for ginger – a cheaper version, no doubt – and red for white wine; and for yellow Syrian food, add blanched fried almonds to the basic ingredients. A Spanish version uses ground pistachio nuts mixed with ground cloves as a substitute for ginger. 'Saracen broth' is a custard made from milk thickened with egg and flavoured with ginger.

There are also recipes for what we would think of as primarily Italian dishes. These manuscripts, indeed, must provide the first written usage in English of the word, if not the concept of, 'pasta'. The first reference to pasta in Italian documents dates from only a few years earlier, although not by the same word – in 1279, 'a basket full of macaroni' is listed among the possessions of a recently deceased merchant. Pasta may well have come from Arab cuisine, since the first description of making pasta is by the

Turk's Head

You will need about 250 grams each of minced pork and minced chicken. Either buy it already ground or pass diced chicken and pork through a mincer. Alternatively, you can simply chop the meat very finely. Put the minced meat into a large bowl and add a few strands of saffron that have soaked for 15 minutes in a thimbleful of warm water. Mix in a teaspoon each of salt and ground cloves and half each of allspice and paprika. Next add two beaten eggs and fresh breadcrumbs from two large slices of white bread. Finally, mix in two tablespoons of ground almonds. All the ingredients should be thoroughly mixed into a large ball. If you can get hold of a pig's stomach, fill it with the mixture. If not, wrap a muslin cloth tightly around the ball, and tie up the loose ends with string. Immerse your encased meatball into boiling water, and cook for about 15 minutes. Test to see whether it is cooked through by sticking a skewer through it. When it is cooked, remove from the water, carefully unwrap and leave to cool a little on a plate. Take three eggs, separate and beat the yolks together, then brush the meat ball all over with the yolks. Put into a medium oven for 4–5 minutes or until golden brown.

Note: For information on obtaining pig stomachs and other such needs, www.Sausage-Casings.co.uk is a good place to start.

Arab geographer al-Idrisi, who saw it being made in Palermo and equated it with an Arab dish, *itriya*.

In the English manuscripts, pasta appears in a rather surprising fashion. In the recipe known as cressee ('criss-cross'), flour and eggs are used to make a dough (the word 'pasta' is used here), which is sweetened with the addition of sugar and ground ginger and coloured with saffron. The pasta is rolled out and cut into strips to form a lattice, then boiled and topped with grated cheese and oil or butter. The recipe for ravioli is perhaps more familiar. Flour, sugar and eggs make a pasta dough. The filling is then formed from a cheese and butter mixture creamed together, to which parsley, sage and finely chopped shallot are added. The ravioli is boiled, then put on a bed of grated cheese, topped with more cheese, and heated again.

Throughout both manuscript collections, we notice a taste for using sweet spices or flavours with meat or in savoury dishes. An example is a fish dish called 'luce in soup'. The fish is parboiled whole, then fried in a pan which has been first rubbed with egg yolk and sprinkled with sugar, and served with onions stewed in wine with saffron. A meatless pottage known as *salmenee* includes vinegar, cinnamon, cloves and ginger, with eggs to thicken it and sugar to balance the spices. A recipe for jellied fish recommends cooking the fish in wine and water with saffron, ginger, cinnamon and galingale. This is a famous recipe, which was used by Chaucer in a love poem in which he compares himself, lost in love, to the fish set in the jelly; galingale seems in this case to be gelatine, although there are versions of the dish in which the fish seems to be braised in spiced wine without gelatine and not to have set. The taste for sweetening savoury dishes with cinnamon, sugar and almond milk is another indication of eastern Mediterranean influence. This was not a case simply of finding uses, however apparently inappropriate, for exotic spices and flavourings in order to show off, for the recipes are similar to ones found in Arabic cookbooks from Baghdad, North Africa and Moorish Spain from the same general period. The increasing availability in the West of spices that had been used for centuries in Eastern cooking led to a revolution in European cooking in the Middle Ages.

Another unusual feature of these recipes is the use of flowers as a food. A recipe for elderflower pottage uses almond milk and wheat starch as thickeners for the broth; the elderflowers are stripped from their stems, rolled in ginger and used as a garnish for the soup. Variations of this recipe use hawthorn blossom or rose petals. It is clear that the flowers were supposed to be an integral part of the dish, and that their taste was valued. The rose petals, for instance, were to be stripped from their centres so as to give a strong flavour. The flowers were not an alternative to a meaty pottage, for both the rose and hawthorn recipes specify the inclusion of pieces of beef, pork or mutton. Elderflowers were also used in a dish called 'white elder', in which chickens are first scalded and then cut into pieces and stewed in almond milk thickened with egg yolk, before the flowers are ground up with salt and added to the dish. Fish can be substituted on a fast day. Although the recipe recommends picking the elderflowers in season, the expectation seems to be that they will be used when dried.

More cookbooks and recipes survive from the fourteenth and fifteenth centuries. We cannot look in detail at all of them, but three French books are worth mentioning, partly because of the influence they had on later cooking and also because of what they tell us about how cooking was viewed as part of the wider picture of household management. The first of these is a book known as *Le Viandier,* written in c.1370 by Guillaume Tirel, chef to the royal French household. Tirel, who is usually known by his rather odd nickname of 'Taillevent' ('wind-slicer' – apparently a reference to the length of his nose), was born in 1310 and died in c.1395. We know that he was employed as a kitchen boy in the household of Jeanne d'Evreux, and that he worked at her coronation feast, before joining the household of Philippe de Valois in 1346. By 1355 he was chef to the dauphin, but later moved to the household of the duke of Normandy and finally, in 1368, became chef to Charles V. On the king's death, he continued to serve the royal household and in 1392 he was made 'Master of the King's Kitchen', a job with responsibility over the provisioning of the whole household.

Le Viandier comprised 133 recipes in its original version, but subsequent editions added recipes until there were 220. The work seems to have owed its origin to King Charles V, who commissioned a series of 'expert guides' to various crafts. Although 'viande' in medieval French referred widely to all foods, not only meat, it is mostly with meat and fish that Taillevant is concerned. All the animals, birds and fish listed earlier in this chapter can be found in

Le Viandier. We can judge the book's popularity in its own day from the number of manuscripts that survive – a clue to the number of times it was copied – and from numerous references to it in later works. It was printed in 1490 and republished a number of times before the eighteenth century, though Taillevant's methods were to be overtaken by the Italian-influenced cuisine brought to France in the household of Catherine de Medici in the sixteenth century.[5]

Le Viandier may be called the first European cookbook in the sense that it is the first text to show a conscious interest in the science of cookery. The stage on which a royal chef such as Taillevant worked his craft, however, was obviously far grander than was usual. In the 1390s, a middle-aged bourgeois Parisian merchant who had married a much younger woman wrote a manual of domestic management for her. This book has come down to us as *Le Menagier of Paris*. Although the names of the author and his wife remain anonymous, the book gives us a vivid window into the bustling household of a prosperous, fussy and rather self-important citizen of Paris in the period of the Hundred Years' War. Surprisingly, perhaps, the basic principles of the cuisine are not so very different from *Le Viandier*, even though the scale is more modest. In both books we can already see a preoccupation with the construction of sauces to accompany meat and fish dishes, or with dishes made from braising and simmering meat.[6]

From a generation or so later comes the book *Du fait de cuisine* by Chiquart Amiczo. Like Taillevant, the author was a 'celebrity chef' of his day – in his case, chef to Count Amadeus VIII of Savoy. However, the purpose of the book is rather different from *Le Viandier* and *Le Menagier*: Amiczo wants to show how a complex variety of dishes can be assembled into a formal banquet; in this respect, he is writing for his own peer group of fellow professionals rather than discoursing on the principles of cooking, like Taillevant, or lecturing his wife on how to run the household, like the author of *Le Menagier*. Amiczo cannot resist showing off his talents, which, as with all kitchen managers working on a grand scale, were as much about organization and logistics as about the preparation of food.

He describes, for example, a feast spread over 2 days comprising 57 separate dishes, for which 100 cows and 100 calves, 130 sheep and 200 lambs, and 120 pigs and 200 piglets were butchered. Beside these quantities of meat, the 2,000 hens hardly raise an eyebrow, though one does wonder how 12,000 eggs could have been consumed on top of all this abundance.

English recipe books begin to emerge properly in the fourteenth century. The best known is *The Forme of Cury on Inglysch*, the first to be written in the English language, but others include *The Noble Boke of Cokery*, *An Ordinance of Pottage* and *Diversa Servicia* (literally, 'Various Menus'). *Cury* provides both the most basic kinds of recipe and more elaborate dishes. For a simple pottage, for example, quarter a cabbage, seethe it in broth, add minced onions and the white parts of leeks, then add saffron, salt and allspice to taste. The eastern Mediterranean influence that we have already noted is still a feature; for example, as in the recipe for 'Viande de Cyprus': Chop up capons and hens into small chunks, heat almond milk in a pot and add ground rice, then add the chopped poultry, sugar, cloves and mace. Bring this to the boil, then take it off the heat and let it stand, before decorating with fried almonds.[7]

Viande de Cyprus

You can use either capon or chicken for this recipe. Skin the fowl and quarter it, then take as much meat off the bone as you can. Alternatively, start with chicken fillets and thighs, chopped into chunks of about an inch each. Heat two cupfuls of almond or coconut milk in a large saucepan. Before it comes to the boil, throw in a cupful of rice, then the chopped fowl, a teaspoon of sugar and half a teaspoon each of whole cloves and ground mace. Bring all this to the boil, then reduce heat and simmer until the rice has absorbed the liquid. Before serving, decorate with fried almonds. Serve either hot or at room temperature.

Generally speaking, these English cookbooks were designed to help professional cooks with responsibilities for designing large and elaborate meals. They typically follow the order of a meal itself, beginning with different kinds of pottages (incidentally, lending force to the theory that pottage was a thin soup rather than a full meal in itself), moving on to fish, poultry, roasted meats, sauces and 'composite' dishes such as rissoles and pies, and finishing with drinks. As with modern cookbooks, there is considerable overlap between these collections, sometimes with only slight differences noticeable in the way individual recipes are presented. These differences may appear greater to a modern reader than they actually were at the time because of the wide variation in spelling in medieval England. The feel of many of the recipes suggests that their authors were not learned scribes copying them for the purposes of establishing a comprehensive collection, but busy professionals who wanted to get their directions across simply and directly. Colloquialisms that must have been common in the kitchen are often used: 'gobbe it small' as an instruction for dicing a piece of beef into cubes is a memorable example. But there are also a number of instructions that are still completely opaque to the modern reader and must either have assumed knowledge of some cooking operations that have been lost to us, or were simply copied down wrong. In the age before printing, of course, copying errors were very frequent and show up in most examples of medieval writing – hardly surprising when one considers the poor light that would have been available to scribes much of the time.

Some of the main features of medieval cuisine are now apparent to us. Spices, especially cinnamon, pepper, ginger and saffron, are used frequently. Sauces are often made by using bread or breadcrumbs as a thickener, where we would use flour or corn starch. Many of the recipes reveal a distinctive medieval taste for combining sweet and savoury tastes in the same dish. To counteract the prevailing sweetness, verjuice (literally, 'green juice') was often used to sharpen the flavour. This was the unsweetened juice of either grapes or crab apples, and seems to have played the role of lemon juice before that fruit became familiar in Europe. Another feature of medieval cuisine is the multiple cooking that was called for in a number of recipes. Meat and fish is often scalded, boiled or simmered before being fried, sautéed or roasted over the fire. A simple example comes from the recipe for 'mock meat' found in both *Le Menagier of Paris* and *Le Viandier*, though with slightly different ingredients in each. Using either leg of lamb (*Le Menagier*) or liver (*Le Viandier*), begin by stewing the meat gently in a broth made half of water and half of dry white wine. When cooked, remove the meat, cut it into small chunks, and sauté these in lard. Add ginger, cinnamon and cloves to the liquid in which the meat cooked, and whisk breadcrumbs into it. Whisk together some egg yolks (the recipe doesn't say how many) and add lemon juice; stir this mixture gently into the broth and simmer until smooth and thick, before returning the sautéed meat to the pot.

One reason for this multiple cooking may have been the concern

---

'Mock meat'

Put half a leg of lamb into a large saucepan containing a mixture of cold water and dry white wine sufficient to cover the joint. Bring to the boil gently, then simmer until the lamb is cooked but still pink inside. Remove the joint, but keep the broth in the saucepan. Cut the meat into small chunks. Heat some lard in a frying pan, then sauté the lamb in it. Next add a teaspoon each of ground ginger, cinnamon and cloves to the broth in which the meat cooked, and put back on a low heat. Add two handfuls of fresh breadcrumbs to the pan, and stir gently. While this is simmering gently, whisk together three egg yolks and a tablespoon of lemon juice; stir this mixture gently into the broth and simmer until it is smooth and thick, before returning the sautéed meat to the pot. Allow the lamb to meld with the sauce for a few minutes before serving.

to ensure that meat was properly cooked all the way through before being eaten, but the technology of the medieval kitchen must also have had something to do with this. Typically, even great kitchens did not make use of ovens. Bread was baked in bread ovens, but cooking of everything else was done over a fire, either in a pot or a flat pan, or roasted. The need to do a lot of cooking in pots over a fire also meant that many recipes result in a dish presented in the form of a sauce or stew. This in turn meant that a variety of thickening agents were used. Flour, which is the commonest such agent in modern cookery, does not seem to have been used for this purpose in medieval cuisine, or at least not in its refined form. Instead, bread was crumbled and stirred into liquids as they cooked. Egg yolks were also popular for this purpose, and ground almonds could be used, especially for dishes with an obviously eastern Mediterranean influence.

Some food historians have remarked on the prevalence of mushy foods as a result of the grinding, pounding and chopping of ingredients that seems to have been required in so many recipes. It has even been suggested that this taste was a deliberate concession to the generally poor state of most people's teeth. Another theory is that because forks were not generally known before the fourteenth century – Edward II is said to have introduced them into England – there was a need for food that could be eaten with a spoon and knife. It is more likely that cooking technology, and the need to cook so much of the food in a pot over an open fire, was the real reason. The lack of an oven, however, did not mean that medieval kitchens could not produce similar results to those we might expect from the technique of casseroling. A recipe for stewed beef in *The Forme of Cury* shows how this can be done by steaming: Put pieces of beef in a jar with chopped onions, whole cloves, mace, currants and some red wine. Ensuring that the jar is stoppered well at the top so that no liquid can get in, stand the jar in a pot of water and bring the pot slowly to the boil, then simmer until the meat is cooked.

It would be a mistake, in any case, to assume that all medieval dishes featured either a thick, soupy gruel or meat roasted on a spit. Considerable sophistication is evident even in dishes that must have been served in bourgeois homes such as that of the author of *Le Menagier of Paris*. There is also a disconcertingly contemporary feel to some recipes. Take, for example, the fourteenth-century French recipe for what is called 'A vinegar and meat appetizer' by its modern editors: Heat a mixture of red wine and beef stock, and whisk in breadcrumbs from two slices of toasted bread. Add two tablespoons of red wine vinegar, ginger, salt and pepper, and a strand of saffron to this sauce. Simmer the whole, then strain. Meanwhile, grill pig's livers (leg of lamb or beef may be substituted), and slice into thin strips. Sauté onions to serve alongside the meat, and pour the sauce over the top. I have eaten starters not dissimilar to this in restaurants influenced by nouvelle cuisine methods.

We can also see in some of these medieval recipes the origins of what would become classical French cuisine. A recipe in Chiquart's *Du fait de cuisine* called 'Jacobin sops', and apparently associated with the Dominican priory in Paris, looks like an early version of a chicken fricassée: Roast a chicken, and when it has cooled, tear the meat off the bones, separating dark from white. Bring to the boil a beef bouillon to which parsley, thyme and marjoram have been added. Lay pieces of toast or reheated bread on the bottom of a wide and shallow casserole, put pieces of soft cheese on top (a cheese like Munster might do very well), then layer the white and dark meat evenly over this, and pour the bouillon over the top. We would probably want to bake this in an oven until the cheese has melted and all the ingredients combined.

MONASTERIES AND MEDIEVAL CUISINE

This chapter has dealt largely with the general context of food and cooking in the Middle Ages. So how much of this applied to monasteries and monastic eating and cooking? Did monastic kitchens follow the trends outlined above in taste and food preparation?

And did cooks in monastic kitchens use the same kinds of recipes as their secular counterparts?

Most food historians regard monasteries from about the middle of the thirteenth century onwards as large communities comparable in their domestic needs to noble households such as those of barons or bishops. Reform monasteries in the Middle Ages, such as the early Cistercian communities and many Byzantine cenobitic monasteries, regarded the preparation and cooking of food as part of the manual service required of monks. This followed the traditional practice of the early monks and monastic founders, who had recommended that such tasks be allocated according to a rota so that every monk took his turn. (None of the sources seem to have considered the possibility that a monk might turn out to be an awful cook – but doubtless that was part of the regime of austerity!) In the mid-twelfth century, Stephen of Obazine took on a lot of the kitchen work in the early days of his new foundation in the forests of the Limousin because he was too frail for other kinds of manual work such as quarrying stone and hauling timber. However, in long-established monasteries, where the abbot kept a separate household, the job of catering for the abbot and his guests was filled by a paid servant.

Some smaller and poorer Benedictine monasteries may still have followed a rota system in preparing food for the refectory, as seems to have been the case, for example, at the convent of Markyate, in Bedfordshire, in the fifteenth century. This certainly did not happen at Cluny, where by 1100 the food was already on a grand scale. Moreover, while a small reforming community of a dozen or so monks could easily manage to share the cooking among themselves, this was obviously not possible when the numbers grew much larger. By the 1060s, Cluny already had three hundred monks, so even if the food had been the simple pottage and bread recommended by St Bernard, it would have required cooking on an industrial scale.

A number of anecdotes in early monastic literature establish a link between service in monastic kitchens, discipline and personal humility. In one version of the *Life of Pachomius,* the great cenobitic founder took on the job of general kitchen servant and cook for the first community that he founded. These connections are echoed in the early Palestinian tradition. According to Cyril of Scythopolis, an Armenian monk called John the Hesychast, who had been a bishop, but who had fled to the Judaean desert to live a simple life of contemplation, asked for the job of kitchen servant when he joined the laura at St Sabas. Similarly, the monk Cyriacus, when turned away from St Euthymius because of his youth, proved himself as a monk by chopping wood and carrying water for the kitchen. In these cases, volunteering for the low-status manual jobs associated with the kitchen was a means of proving oneself in the cenobium.[8]

These stories also remind us that kitchen work was often physically demanding. A twelfth-century monk of St Sabas, Gabriel, was possessed by demons when he tried a spell of solitary living on a column in the desert. In order to rid him of the demons when he returned to the laura, the abbot prescribed a regime of manual labour in the form of fetching and carrying fuel for the kitchen and bakery. This would have required considerable strength, and was supposed to be physically exhausting for Gabriel. Each load, says the author of the anecdote, was like the cargo borne by a camel on its back: 'You could see this man every day bringing a load of wood on his shoulders hardly less than a camel's load . . . he was in subjection, slaving away zealously in the monastery.'[9] Providing the wood for the kitchens of a medioval monastery in England or France might not mean toiling in the heat of the desert in quite the same way, but the quantities of fuel required for a large kitchen were very considerable. Kitchens therefore needed servants to do this kind of menial labour, besides those who did the cooking.

We know very little, unfortunately, about cooks in medieval monasteries. As we have seen, overall charge of the commissariat was given to a monk, the cellarer. It was he who had the responsibility for ensuring a supply of provisions, and the cook and kitchen staff must have all come under his direction. He may also have had the final say about choosing the menus, since we know that he was responsible for finding out what diets the monks in the infirmary had been prescribed and providing them. In some monasteries in the twelfth century, such as Abingdon, the cook seems also to have been a monk – or at least, the monk with responsibility for the kitchen is given the title *coquinarius*. A monastery in which the *Rule of Benedict* was observed strictly to the letter scarcely provided challenges for a cook, since he would have been required to pro-duce the same pottage and vegetable-based diet day after day. But as communities found ways around the dietary restrictions in the *Rule*, the range of foods that was deemed appropriate widened considerably, and cellarers must surely have left more of the choice about what foods to prepare to professional cooks.

Even small monasteries seem to have employed cooks. At Lanercost Priory, an Augustinian monastery on the Scottish border near Carlisle, the cook named in a fourteenth-century charter had started serving the abbey as a 'kitchen groom' when only a boy. Lanercost probably never had more than fifteen or so monks at any one time, but even so, a staff including a head cook and under-lings was clearly regarded as normal. Augustinian houses did not have to observe the same culinary discipline, even in principle, as Benedictine. The keynote of the Augustinian *Rule* was moderation in all things. Neither self-indulgence nor self-denial was to be taken to extremes, and meat was not prohibited.

However, developments in thirteenth-century monasteries were probably crucial in bringing about changes in the kitchens of many Benedictine monasteries. Once the Church had accepted the slackening of the *Rule* in respect of diet by recognizing the existence of misericords and permitting meat and other dishes not specified in the *Rule* to be eaten outside the refectory, it was obvi-ously necessary for monasteries to be able to provide what monks were demanding, and this meant a larger kitchen staff to cook a wider variety of dishes. Certainly, what we know of menus in some monasteries in the later Middle Ages suggests not only that they employed kitchen staff on the same scale as a great secular household, but also that the food they ate was very similar to the kinds of dishes described in this chapter. On one Sunday in 1381, the Norwich Cathedral Priory monks sat down to sucking-pig, beef, chicken and moyle (warm bread soaked in the juices of roast meat). At St Swithun's, Winchester, on 13 July 1493, the monks ate moyle, eggs (280 of them were used!), morterells (meatballs made of chicken or another poultry), beef and mutton. We do not know how the meats were prepared, but recipes for morterells are common in medieval cookery books. These records, though admittedly not necessarily to be taken as typical of daily fare, suggest that kitchens at wealthy monasteries were producing food of the same type as in important secular households.

Morterells

The quantities in this recipe are designed for a small community of about 12 monks, but it can easily be adapted for bigger houses. However many sausages you use, you will need about half that quantity of dried breadcrumbs.

Finely chop four onions and six cloves of garlic. Take two dozen sausages and either split open the casing of each with a sharp knife or squeeze out the meat from one end, and collect in a large bowl. Mix the sausage meat and onion together thoroughly, then add breadcrumbs. Add a good handful of chopped parsley, a little salt, ground pepper or paprika and ground cinnamon When all is well mixed, shape the mixture into little balls. Bring a pot of water to the boil, throw the sausage balls in and reduce the heat. Allow to simmer gently for 6 minutes, then remove the balls from water. (Note: It is important to keep the water simmering – if it is boiling too rapidly, the mortadels will fall apart.) Heat a couple of tablespoons of oil or lard in a frying pan, and fry the balls gently in the fat, stirring them around but making sure they retain their shape. When they turn golden brown, they are ready.

Conclusion

The earliest monks were solitaries: individuals disillusioned with their world to the point of dropping everything in order to live on the margins of human society. They lived in caves, in abandoned ruins in deserted regions, in purpose-built cells, or under the stars. Some banded together for safety or for mutual support. At the same time, some gave free rein to entrepreneurial tendencies by organizing themselves into communities, and colonizing deserted places. Eventually, living a religious life in a community became the norm among monks, and solitaries the exception. Monasteries developed in different ways in different parts of the late Roman world, according to local environment, climate and regional traditions. Some monasteries, such as the laura communities in Palestine and, centuries later, the Carthusians in the medieval West, succeeded in combining solitary monasticism with communal organization.

Solitary monasticism never completely died out; indeed, during a vigorous period of reform beginning in the eleventh century, hermits and anchorites came into vogue once again. This was the great age of monastic revivalism, in which new foundations seemed to be springing up everywhere one looked, and hermits and monks populated forests, wildernesses and uncultivated waste ground throughout Europe and the Near East. Monks, nuns, hermits and holy men appeared in bewildering variety, some following set rules or formulae for living, some adapting or inventing their own, and some apparently following no rule at all. Some lived in communities for a time, then drifted off to live by themselves or to gather another like-minded group together to found a new community. Such a fluid situation couldn't last. By the later Middle Ages all monasticism, both solitary and communal, was tightly organized and regulated. Solitaries were required to register with their bishop and to follow a personal regime directed by him. Both in the 'golden age' of the early centuries and in the revival of monasticism, monks and hermits had sometimes been interchangeable, as religious-minded men and women explored different ways of leading a spiritual life. But by about 1300, such fluidity was no longer encouraged; in fact, the Church cracked down on it because of the fear of heresy and unorthodoxy. Monastic life continued to flourish and even to find new forms of expression: in the Catholic West, the coming of the friars in the thirteenth century represented a new kind of spiritual reform, and in the Byzantine world, the later Middle Ages saw the efflorescence of *hesychasm*, a mystical movement that emphasized repetitive prayer and stillness.

Monastic life embraced paradox. From the very beginning, monks wanted above all to escape the burdens of living in human society. They sought freedom from social and family obligations and ties by retreating to the desert, wilderness and forest. To Neophytos the Recluse, the founder of the cave monastery of the Enkleistra in Cyprus in the twelfth century, the monastery was a refuge from the sordid dramas of village life – the yoke and the noose of a wretched existence, as he bitterly remarked. Poverty, bereavement and sudden, inescapable calamity – this, for him, was life outside the monastery. But it was impossible even for the cave-dwelling Neophytos to escape being human. Monks might try to recreate a paradise within their walls, or in the cloister, or even in a dry desert wadi, but they could never find a refuge from their own humanity. They might wish to become like the angels, but while they still lived on earth, they needed to eat, and what they ate had both practical and symbolic implications.

Examining monastic life through food – what was eaten and how it was cooked, and how it arrived in the kitchen in the first place – gives us insights into what those who chose this life thought about their own humanity. The question of why certain foods were favoured and others avoided offers a constant reminder of the monks' human limitations. It would be easy to see the history of monasticism in this way as a story of failure, or at least of disappointed hopes. The earliest monks appear – at least as we meet them in the sources – as heroes, 'athletes' of asceticism, with the spiritual strength and self-discipline to overcome their bodily needs and survive on the bare minimum of food. In contrast with the monks of Nitria and Scete, Sabas and his laura dwellers in the wadis of Palestine, the fervent Symeon the Stylite and his terrifying self-denial, or their later successors in the forests of western France and the moors of northern England, the Benedictine monks of the later Middle Ages must appear to us soft and complacent, doing little but eating and drinking, and devoting much of their time to thinking up ways of dodging the hard rules set for them by their founding fathers.

There is doubtless some truth in this. It was easier to be a monk in fifteenth-century England than in fifth-century Syria. But the reason for this is not only because weaker, less heroic individuals became monks – and still less because 'the Church' as an institution was in decline. Monasticism became an easier life because it had changed fundamentally in order to accommodate the needs of human society outside the monastery. What began as rejection of society became an expression of the aspirations of that society. If monks could not entirely escape the outside world, that world came to realize that it needed monks: it needed their learning and knowledge, it needed their employment and their production capabilities, and above all it needed their spiritual protection. But in needing these things, the world also came to rely on precisely that feature of monasteries that can appear to us as a mark of their failure to live up to their own ideals. Monasteries could only thrive if they could become powerful, self-sufficient organizations, capable of feeding and clothing large communities – and doing this successfully meant paying attention to dimensions of human life that might seem far removed from their original purpose.

It is difficult not to find the desert fathers impressive. Even if we cannot understand or empathize with it, their determination to perfect themselves through neglecting their bodily needs merits our admiration. Admiring the monks of several centuries later who enjoyed the same kind of feasts as the rich outside the cloister is more difficult. But in the end there is a distance between us and the monks of the 'golden age' that cannot be explained simply by the passing of centuries. There were, doubtless, always monks in every age who observed rules about eating and fasting strictly and who were no less ascetic than the desert fathers. But the monks who thought up ways around the *Rule of Benedict* so as to be able to eat meat sometimes, or who hid honey from their fellows, or who could not stand another day of eating bean stew, are in the end more familiar to us. Enjoying and taking an interest in what we eat is, after all, only human.

Notes

Notes to Chapter One: Beginnings – who were the first monks?

1 Guibert de Nogent's memoirs were translated into English by J. F. Benton (1984) as *Self and Society in Medieval France*. Toronto: University of Toronto Press.

2 D. Burton-Christie (1993), *The Word in the Desert: Scripture and the Quest for Holiness in Early Christian Monasticism*. UK: Oxford University Press, pp. vii–viii.

3 *Palladius: the Lausiac History*, trans. Robert T. Meyer (1965), Westminster, MD: Newman Press, p. 86; *The Life of Antony by Athanasius*, in Carolinne White (1998) *Early Christian Lives*. Harmondsworth: Penguin, 1998, p. 13. For the story of Onuphrios, see Tim Vivian (1993) *Histories of the Monks of Upper Egypt and the Life of Onuphrios*. Kalamazoo: Cistercian Publications.

4 *Life of Symeon the Holy Fool*, in D. Kreuger (1996), *Symeon the Holy Fool: Leontius' Life and the Late Antique City*. Berkeley: University of California Press, p. 132

Notes to Chapter Two: Desert fathers, pillar-saints and fasting

1 Jerome, 'Life of Hilarion', in C. White (trans.) (1997), *Early Christian Lives*. Harmondsworth, UK: Penguin, pp. 93–4.

2 *Palladius: the Lausiac History*, pp. 58–9.

3 Dioscorus, Sisoes, Macarius and Arsenius, see B. Ward, (trans.) (1984), *The Sayings of the Desert Fathers*. Kalamazoo: Cistercian Publications, pp. 55, 212–22, 124–38, 9–19. Isaiah, see E. A. Wallis Budge (1907), *Paradise of the Holy Fathers*, vol. 2. London: Chatto and Windus, p. 16.

4 *Palladius: the Lausiac History*, pp 58–9.
5 *Paradise of the Holy Fathers*, vol. 2, p. 16.
6 *The Sayings of the Fathers*, 29; *Cyril of Scythopolis*, translated by Richard Price (1991), *Lives of the Monks of Palestine*. Kalamazoo: Cistercian Publications, p. 140.
7 Ephrem the Syrian, 'Second Sermon on the Deceased Fathers', in C. Emereau (1918–19) *Saint Ephrem le Syrien, son oeuvre littéraire grecque*. Paris: Maison de la bonne presse, pp. 40–9. Sozomen, *Historia Ecclesiastica*, VI, 32. *Life of Symeon the Holy Fool*, in D. Kreuger (1996), *Symeon the Holy Fool: Leontius' Life and the Late Antique City*. Berkeley: University of California Press, p. 141.
8 N. Russell (trans.) (1981), *The Lives of the Desert Fathers (Historia Monachorum in Aegypto)*. Kalamazoo: Cistercian Publications, p. 71.
9 'Life of Euthymius', in *Cyril of Scythopolis*, translated by Richard Price (1991), *Lives of the Monks of Palestine*. Kalamazoo: Cistercian Publications, pp. 11, 17, 53, 108.
10 C. Doughty, edited by H. L. MacRitchie (1989), *Arabia Deserta*. London: Bloomsbury/Phillips & Company, p. 68.
11 James of Nisibis, see Theodoret, *Historia Religiosa*, 27.1.
12 Matt Larsen (2009), *US Army Survival Handbook*. Guildford, CT: Globe Piquot Press, pp. 150–60.
13 John Moschus, translated by J. Wortley (1992), *The Spiritual Meadow*. Kalamazoo, Cistercian Publications, chap. 129.
14 C. Doughty, *Arabia Deserta*, p. 65.
15 James of Vitry: see F. Moschus (ed.), *Historia Orientalis*, LIII, 87–80. Reginald of Durham, see Surtees Society (1847), *Libellus sancti Godrici*, X, pp. 42–3.
16 John the Dwarf, see B. Ward (trans.) (1975), *Sayings of the Desert Fathers*. Kalamazoo: Cistercian Publications, p. 86.
17 *Life of Symeon the Holy Fool*, p. 153. The many anecdotes illustrating Symeon's extraordinary behaviour are on pp. 150–69.
18 Josephus, translated by H. St J. Thackeray (1961), *Jewish War*, vol. II. Cambridge MA: Loeb Classical Library, pp. 119–62.
19 *Paradise of the Holy Fathers*, vol. 2, p. 23 John Cassian, *Conferences*, vol. II, 17–22.
20 *Paradise of the Holy Fathers*, vol. 2, p. 16.
21 *Paradise of the Holy Fathers*, vol. 2, p. 104.
22 'Life of Sabas', in *Cyril of Sycthopolis*, translated by R. M. Price (1991),

The Lives of the Monks of Palestine. Kalamazoo: Cistercian Publications, p. 169. 'Rule of Pachomius', in *Patrologia Latina*, 23, cols 65–86.

23 Herbert of Clairvaux, *Liber Miraculorum*, PL 185, cols 1223–4.

24 For the estimate of the number of monks served by seven bakeries, see *Palladius: Lausiac History*, pp. 40–1. For the story of Sabas and the oven, see 'Life of Sabas', in *Lives of the Monks of Palestine*, pp. 97–8.

25 For Pachomius' rules for the bakery, see the version of the *Rule of Pachomius* in *Pachomian Koinonia II*, CSCO 46, p. 163.

26 A. Veillaux (trans.), *Bohairic Life of Pachomius*, CSCO 45, pp. 100–4.

27 The Onuphrios story, as told by the monk Paphnutios, is in Vivian (1993), *Histories of the Monks of Upper Egypt and Life of Onuphrios*.

Notes to Chapter Three: The 'hermit craze' of the Middle Ages

1 The document can be read in an English translation in E. F. Henderson (1910), *Select Historical Documents of the Middle Ages*. London: George Bell and Sons, pp. 329–33.

2 J. F. Benton (1984), *Self and Society in Medieval France*. Toronto: Medieval Academy of America, pp. 53–4.

3 The episode is reprinted from the '*Historia Ecclesiastica* of Orderic Vitalis', in E. R. Elder (1998), *The New Monastery. Texts and Studies on the Earliest Cistercians*. Kalamazoo: Cistercian Publications, pp. 19–25.

4 Bernard's letter to Robert is translated in B. S. James (1998), *The Letters of St Bernard of Clairvaux*. Stroud: Sutton, pp. 1–10.

5 Much of Bernard's Apologia to Abbot William has been reprinted in P. Matarasso (ed.) (1993), *The Cistercian World*. Harmondsworth: Penguin, pp. 44–58. The treatise can also be read in full in Michael Casey (ed.) (1970), *Cistercians and Cluniacs, Cistercian Fathers Series*, vol. 1. Kalamazoo: Cistercian Publications, pp. 52–7.

6 Gerald of Wales, Autobiography, pp. 70–2.

7 The description of St Bernard from the Vita Prima is in P. Matarasso (ed.), *The Cistercian World*. Harmondsworth: Penguin pp. 38–9. Elias of Narbonne is one of the hermits described in Gerard of Nazareth (1562–74), 'Matthias Falcius Illyricus', *Duodecima Centuria*, vol. 6. of *Ecclesiasticae Historia*, 7 vols. Basel, cols 1608–9.

8 Walter Daniel, edited and translated by F. M. Powicke (1950), *Life of Ailred of Rievaulx*. London: Thomas Nelson: p. 11. Also reprinted

in P. Matarasso (ed.) (1993), *The Cistercian World*. Harmondsworth: Penguin, pp. 153–4. For Benedict's stipulations on food, see T. Fry (ed.) (1982), *The Rule of St Benedict in English*. Collegeville, MI: Liturgical Press, pp. 61–3.

9   W. Macray (ed.) (1863), *Chronicon abbatiae de Evesham*. London: HMSO, Rolls Series, pp. 103–5, 237–40. The Whitby incident is in W. A. Pantin (ed.), *Documents Illustrating the Activities of the General and Provincial Chapters of the English Black Monks 1215–1540*. Camden Society 3rd series, 45–47, vol. 1, p. 259.

10   J. P. Thomas and A. Hero (eds) (2000), *Byzantine Monastic Foundation Documents*. Washington DC: Dumbarton Oaks, pp. 395–8.

11   N. Coureas (trans.) (2003), *The Foundation Rules of Medieval Cypriot Monasteries: Makhairas and St Neophytos*. Nicosia: Cyprus Research Centre, p. 160.

12   Quoted from 'Prodromic Poems' by A. Dalby (2003), *Flavours of Byzantium*. Totnes, UK: Prospect Books, p. 94.

13   P. Squatriti (trans.) (2007), *The Complete Works of Liutprand of Cremona*. Washington DC: Catholic University of America Press, p. 187; E. R. Sewter (ed. and trans.) (1969), *The Alexiad of Anna Comnena*. Harmondsworth. UK: Penguin, p. 103

14   Evergetis 10, trans. Robert Jordan, in (2000) *Byzantine Monastic Foundation Documents*, Washington DC: Dumbarton Oaks, pp. 480–1.

15   For regulations at Makhairas, see *The Foundation Rules of Medieval Cypriot Monasteries*, Nicosia: Cyprus Research Centre, pp. 92–4. For the laura of Athanasios, see *Byzantine Monastic Foundation Documents*, pp. 226–7.

16   R. Greenfield (ed. and trans.) (2000), *Life of Lazaros of Mount Galesion*. Washington DC: Dumbarton Oaks, 2000), pp. 122, 125, 141–2, 169–73.

17   Lawrence Durrell (2009) *Prospero's Cell*. Olympia Press. New Traveller's Companion Series 139. P.110

18   P. Matarasso (ed.) (1993), *The Cistercian World*. Harmondsworth, UK: Penguin, pp. 300–1.

19   *Byzantine Monastic Foundation Documents*, pp. 691–2 (Douka), 746–7 (Pantokrator).

20   There is an English translation of the Godric story in H. Waddell (1934), *Beasts and Saints*. London: Constable, pp. 84–6.

21   Thomas of Celano, *The Remembrance of the Desire of a Soul*, pp. 216–17.

22 Details are in S. F. Hockey, *The Account Book of Beaulieu Abbey*, Camden Society Publications, series 4, 16 (1976), pp. 1–348.
23 P. Matarasso (ed.) (1993), *The Cistercian World*. Harmondsworth, UK: Penguin, p. 31.
24 Bruce Venarde (2003) *Robert of Arbrissel. A Medieval Religious Life*, Washington DC: Catholic University of America Press, pp. 12–16.
25 M. Aubrun (ed.) (1970), *Vie de Saint Etienne d'Obazine*. Clermont-Ferrand:Publications de l'Institut d'études du Massif Central, pp. 42–106.
26 *Duodecima Centuria*, cols 1603–10.

Notes to Chapter Four: Herbs and health

1 *Sancti Bernardi Opera* (1977) ed. H. Rochais, C. H. Talbot and J. Leclercq. 8 vols. Turnhout: Brepols. vol 8. *Epistolae*, p. 287.
2 Dublin, Trinity College MS 370, fos 48v–49r, for charms and recipes using herbs.
3 Some Byzantine texts on the humours and the qualities of foods have been assembled and translated into English by A. Dalby (2003), *Flavours of Byzantium*. London, UK: Prospect Books, pp. 132–60.
4 L. C. Arano (trans. and ed.) (1992), *The Medieval Health Handbook: Tacinium Sanitatis*. New York: George Braziller.
5 S. Weber (ed.) (1924) *Anthimus, De Observatio Ciborum*. Leiden, The Netherlands: E. J. Brill Ltd.
6 P. Gray (2002), *Honey from a Weed*. Totnes, UK: Prospect Books, p. 201. The piece by Elizabeth David was originally published (1979) in *Herbal Review*, and reprinted (1984) in *An Omelette and a Glass of Wine*. UK: Penguin, pp. 106–9.
7 R. Mabey (2004), *Flora Britannica Book of Wild Herbs*. London, UK: Sinclair-Stevenson Ltd, p. 110.
8 John Gardener's treatise was edited by A. Amherst (1895) in *Archaeologia*, LIV, pp. 157–72. We should note, however, that some plants, such as foxglove (Digitalis) might be recognized as having a medicinal use while also being naturally poisonous, and for this reason some monastic herb gardens used a system of raised beds to segregate plants.

Notes to Chapter Five: From field to table – the medieval monastic experience

1 Sulpicius Severus, *Dialogues*, I, 13, in (1894), *Select Library of Nicene and Post-Nicene Fathers of the Christian Church*, ed. Henry Wace, vol. 11. UK: Oxford, p. 30.

2 The description of Clairvaux is in P. Matarasso (ed.) (1993), *The Cistercian World*. Harmondsworth, UK: Penguin, pp. 287–92. Gerald of Wales' comments on Cistercian and Cluniac land management can be found in L. Thorpe (trans.) (1978), *Journey Through Wales and Description of Wales*. Harmondsworth, UK: Penguin, pp. 105–7.

3 *Farming and Gardening in Late Medieval Norfolk: Norwich Cathedral Priory Gardener's Accounts 1329–1530*, ed. C. Noble, C. Moreton, P. Rutledge, Norfolk Record Society vol 16 (1996).

4 H. E. Butler (trans. and ed.) (1949), *The Chronicle of Jocelyn of Brakelond*. London: Nelson, pp. 5–7, 89. The account of the cellarer's duties is on pages 102–4.

5 Anon, *Paradise of the Fathers*, vol. 2. pp. 79–80.

6 W. Macray (ed.) (1863), *Chronicon abbatiae de Evesham*. London: HMSO, Rolls Series, pp. 103–5, 237–40. *Chronicon abbatiae de Evesham*, p. 189.

7 J. P. Thomas and A. Hero (eds) (2000), *Byzantine Monastic Foundation Documents*. Washington DC: Dumbarton Oaks, pp. 480, 499. The monastery was the Mother of God Evergetis, in the suburbs of Constantinople.

8 Thomas of Elmham, *Historia monasterii sancti Augustini Cantuarensis*, p. 55.

9 B. Harvey (1993), *Living and Dying in England*, 1100–1540. Oxford, UK: Oxford University Press, pp. 38–67.

10 Thomas, J. P. and Hero, A. (eds) (2000), *Byzantine Monastic Foundation Documents*, [Eleousa]. Washington DC: Dumbarton Oaks, pp. 175–6, 183–4.

11 Eadmer, see R. W. Southern (trans. and ed.) (1962), *Life of St Anselm*. London, UK: Thomas Nelson and Sons Ltd, p. 78. This describes charmingly Anselm's modest eating habits as abbot, and his custom of inviting selected monks to his table for spiritual conversation.

12 *The Chronicle of Jocelyn of Brakelond*, pp. 39–40.

Notes to Chapter Six: Medieval diets – the food landscape

1 Christopher Dyer (1989) *Standards of Living in the Later Middle Ages. Social Change in England c.1200–1520*, pp. 49–85.

2 John Harvey, 'Vegetables in the Middle Ages', *Garden History* 12 (1984), 89–99, provides a full discussion of pottage.

3 For this anecdote from Usamah ibn Munqidh's 'autobiography', see P. K. Hitti (trans.) (1929), *Memoirs of an Arab-Syrian Gentleman and Warrior*. Princeton: Princeton University Press, pp. 169–70. The autobiography has been re-issued very many times since, with the most recent English translation being Paul Cobb's (2008), *The Book of Contemplation*. Harmondsworth, UK: Penguin.

4 C. B. Hieatt and R. F. Jones (1986), 'Two Anglo-Norman Culinary Collections Edited from British Library Manuscripts Additional 32085 and Royal 12.C.xii', *Speculum*, 61, 859–82.

5 T. Scully (ed.) (1988), *The Viander of Taillevent*. Ottawa: University of Ottawa.

6 G. Greco and C. Rose (trans.) (2009), *Good Wife's Guide: A Medieval Household Book*. Ithaca: Cornell.

7 C. B. Hieatt and S. Butler (eds) (1985), *Curye on Inglysch: English Culinary Manuscripts of the Fourteenth Century*, Early English Text Society, supplementary series 8. London, UK: Oxford University Press. More early English recipes have been collected in C. Hieatt (2008), *A Gathering of Medieval English Recipes*. Turnhout: Brepols.

8 Cyril of Scythopolis, *Lives of the Monks of Palestine*, pp. 224, 247.

9 'Narratio de monacho Palestinensis', in H. Delehaye (ed.) (1907), *Saints de Chypre*. Analecta Bollandiana, 26, 62–75.

Further Reading

General works on food and food history are plentiful, but not all of them are accurate or helpful for the medieval period. The best general guides are Alan Davidson's *The Oxford Companion to Food* (Oxford: OUP, 1999) and the *Larousse Gastronomique* (Paris: Larousse, 2007; English edition, London: Hamlyn, 2009). I also found Maguelonne Toussaint-Samat's books stimulating, especially *Histoire naturelle et morale de la nourriture* (Paris: Bordas, 1987). On olives, *Olives. The Life and Lore of a Noble Fruit* by Mort Rosenblum (New York: Absolute Press, 1996) was very useful. Mention should also be made of the inspirational and entertaining *Extreme Cuisine* by Jerry Hopkins (Hong Kong: Periplus, 2004).

There are several studies of the early history of monasticism in the eastern Mediterranean. The classic study in English is Derwas Chitty's *The Desert a City* (Oxford: Blackwell, 1966), but more recent guides have been written by Marilyn Dunn, *The Emergence of Monasticism* (Oxford: Blackwell, 2000), and William Harmless, *Desert Christians. An Introduction to the Literature of Early Monasticism* (Oxford: OUP, 2004). Philip Rousseau's *Ascetics, Authority and the Church in the Age of Jerome and Cassian* (Oxford: OUP, 1978) is perhaps less accessible for a general audience than his *Pachomius: The Making of a Community in Fourth-Century Egypt* (Berkeley: University of California Press, 1999). James Goehring's essay 'The Origins of Monasticism', reprinted in his *Ascetics, Society and the Desert: Studies in Egyptian Monasticism* (Harrisburg: Trinity Press International, 1993), is an excellent specialist introduction to Egyptian monasticism. For a good introduction to the early Church in general, *The Early Church* by Henry Chadwick (Harmondsworth, UK: Penguin, 1993), is a good starting-point, while W. H. C. Frend's

The Rise of Christianity (London: Darton, Longman and Todd, 1984) provides exhaustive detail on almost every aspect. Robin Lane Fox's *Pagans and Christians* (Harmondsworth, UK: Penguin, 1986) is a more contentious guide to the background of early Christianity. Joseph Patrich writes more specifically on laura monasticism in *Sabas, Leader of Palestinian Monasticism* (Washington DC: Dumbarton Oaks, 1995). For Syria, the classic work is by Arthur Voobus, *History of Asceticism in the Syrian Orient*, 3 volumes (Louvain: CSCO, 1960–88). For the West, Conrad Leyser's *Authority and Asceticism from Augustine to Gregory the Great* (Oxford: OUP, 2000) is a scholarly examination of the theme of asceticism in general. Another valuable study of asceticism in this period is by Peter Brown, *The Body and Society: Men, Women and Sexual Renunciation in Early Christianity* (London: Faber, 1990). Mayeul de Dreuille's *The Rule of St Benedict and the Ascetic Traditions from Asia to the West* (Leominster: Gracewing, 2000) places the *Rule* in a broad context of ascetic guides to living.

Many of the contemporary works of the 'golden age' of monasticism can be read in English translation. Athanasius' *Life of Anthony* is available in a number of English versions, the most recent being in the Cistercian Studies series, translated by Tim Vivian, Apostolos Athanassakis and Rowan Greer (Kalamazoo, MI: Cistercian Studies, 2003). The 'alphabetical version' of the *Sayings of the Fathers* was translated by Benedicta Ward (London: Macmillan, 1980). Cyril of Scythopolis' biographies of Sabas and other Palestinian monks have been translated by Richard Price as *Lives of the Monks of Palestine* (Kalamazoo, MI: Cistercian Studies, 1991). Richard Price also translated Theoderet of Cyrrhus' *History of the Monks of Syria* (Kalamazoo, MI: Cistercian Studies, 1988), which is the main contemporary source for the career of Symeon the Stylite. There has not been an English translation of Palladius' *Lausiac History* for many years, but Dom Cuthbert Butler's version (Cambridge: CUP, 1898–1904) is still valuable. I have used the translation by Robert Meyer, *Palladius: the Lausiac History*, in the Ancient Christian Writers series (London: Longman, 1965).

John Cassian's *Conferences* are available in a French translation in the Sources Chrétiennes series, no. 64 (Paris: Cerf, 1964), and in English at www.osb.org/lectio/cassian/conf/index.html. Saint Basil's ascetic works were translated by W. K. Lowther Clarke (London: SPCK, 1925), and this is still the most accessible English version. John Moschus' *Spiritual Meadow* has been translated by John Wortley (Kalamazoo, MI: Cistercian Studies, 1992). *The Life of Symeon the Holy Fool* was translated by Derek Kreuger as an appendix to his book *Symeon the Holy Fool: Leontius' Life and the Late Antique City* (Berkeley, CA: University of California Press, 1996). The *Rule of St Benedict* is readily available in a large number of English versions, both in print and online. A recent version is the translation by the monks of Glenstal Abbey (Blackrock: Four Courts Press, 1994). The website www.osb.org, besides offering translations into a number of different modern languages, also points readers in the direction of further studies.

The tradition of early Irish monasticism is well trodden ground. A good introduction is offered by John Ryan in *Irish Monasticism: Origins and Early Development*, first published in 1931 but more recently reissued (Shannon: Irish University Press, 1972). The flavour of the literary culture of early medieval monasticism can be tasted in Helen Waddell's classic *The Wandering Scholars* (London: Constable, 1927). St Columbanus is the subject of a very recent study by Carol Richards (Exeter: Imprint Academic, 2010).

The best short study of medieval monasticism in most of its aspects is C. H. Lawrence's *Medieval Monasticism*, (London: Longman, 1984). A more recent work covering the same ground but for Britain alone is Janet Burton's *The Monastic and Religious Orders in Britain, 1000–1300* (Cambridge: CUP, 2007), but the classic work is by David Knowles, *The Monastic Order in England* (Cambridge: CUP, 1940). David Williams's *The Cistercians in the Early Middle Ages* (Leominster: Gracewing, 1998) has excellent discussions of the practical economy of medieval monasticism. There is a wealth of scholarly literature on Cluny, but a good introductory guide to what it was like to be a Cluniac monk can be found in Joan

Evans's *Monastic Life at Cluny 910–1157* (Oxford: OUP, 1968). A more recent book that summarizes much of the scholarly literature is Edwin Mullins's *In Search of Cluny: God's Lost Empire* (Signal, 2006). Specifically on the reform movement in western monasticism, Henrietta Leyser's *Hermits and the New Monasticism* (New York: St Martin's, 1984) deals with the 'return to the desert' in the late eleventh and early twelfth centuries. Bernard of Clairvaux has been the subject of many studies, one of the classics being Watkin Williams's *Saint Bernard of Clairvaux* (Manchester: MUP, 1935), and one of the more recent Adriaan Bredero's *Saint Bernard. Between Cult and History* (Grand Rapids, MI: Eerdmans, 1996). A very useful collection of contemporary Cistercian writing is *The Cistercian World*, edited by Pauline Matarasso (Harmondsworth, UK: Penguin, 1993). This includes sections from the *First Life* of St Bernard, the contemporary biography that includes an intimate description of the abbot. Bernard's diatribe against monastic excesses, the 'Apology to Abbot William', is available in an English translation by Michael Casey as *Cistercians and Cluniacs* (Kalamazoo, MI: Cistercian Studies, 1987). For later medieval monastic life, the classic study – excellent in all respects and especially valuable for food – is Barbara Harvey's *Living and Dying in England. The Monastic Experience 1100–1540* (Oxford: OUP, 1993).

Study of Byzantine monasticism has been greatly facilitated by the publication of *Byzantine Monastic Foundation Documents* in five volumes, edited by Angela Hero and John Thomas (Washington DC: Dumbarton Oaks, 2000), which comprises the typika of a large number of foundations between the seventh and sixteenth centuries. Byzantine food and eating is the preserve of Andrew Dalby, whose *Flavours of Byzantium* (Totnes, UK: Prospect, 2003) is indispensable. Patricia Skinner has made a good study of food and health in a regional context in *Health and Medicine in Early Medieval Southern Italy* (Leiden, The Netherlands: Brill, 1997). In a similar vein, but with a broader brief, is Massimo Livi-Bacci's seminal work of social anthropology, *Population and Nutrition* (Cambridge: CUP, 1991).

Food history is now a recognized branch of medieval studies. A scholarly article by M. Dembinska, 'Diet: A Comparison of Food Consumption between some Eastern and Western Monasteries in the 4th–12th Centuries', in *Byzantion*, 55, (1985, 431–62), exemplifies a number of more specific studies on the history of food production and food economy, many of which can be found in the volumes of the *Oxford Symposium on Food and Cookery*, edited by Harlan Walker for Prospect Books from 1983 onward. A more scholarly collection is *Food in Medieval England. Diet and Nutrition*, edited by D. Serjeantson, C. M. Woolgar and T. Waldron (Oxford: OUP, 2006). There is also a useful discussion in Christopher Dyer's *Standards of Living in the Later Middle Ages* (Cambridge: CUP, 1989). John Harvey's work on medieval gardens and gardening, especially the article 'Vegetables in the Middle Ages', in *Garden History, 12* (1984, 89–99), is also valuable, while *Medieval English Gardens* by Teresa McLean (London: Collins, 1981) is both readable and learned. The doyen of scholars of medieval cookery and cookbooks is Terence Scully, whose *The Art of Cookery in the Middle Ages* (Woodbridge: Boydell, 1995) is the fundamental work. Scully has also translated Chicquart's *On Cookery* (New York: P. Lang, 1986). The most recent version of *Le Menagier de Paris* is the *Good Wife's Guide: A Medieval Household Book*, translated by Gina Greco and Christine Rose (Ithaca: Cornell, 2009), but an earlier discussion, in Eileen Power's *Medieval People* (London: Routledge, 1928), is still worth reading. Also worthy of mention is Toby Peterson's article 'The Arab Influence on western European Cooking', in *Journal of Medieval History*, 6 (1980, 317–40). A good general book on spices is by Andrew Dalby, *Dangerous Tastes* (London: British Museum, 2000).

The literature on herbs and herbals is too extensive to explore thoroughly here. I found the classic collection by Geoffrey Grigson, *The Englishman's Flora* (London: Phoenix, 1968) full of wisdom and insight. The books by Richard Mabey, *Flora Britannica Guide to Wild Herbs* (London: Chatto and Windus, 1998) and *Food for Free* (London: Collins, 1972) were very useful reference works. There is a chapter on weed eating in Patience Gray's excellent *Honey from a Weed* (Totnes, UK: Prospect Books, 2002).

Index